OPTIONS TRADING

QuickStart Guide

SECOND EDITION

The Simplified Beginner's Guide To Options Trading

ClydeBank
FINANCE

Edition # 2 – Created : July 19, 2018

Editors : Marilyn Burkley and Patricia Guth

Cover Illustration and Design: Katie Poorman, Copyright © 2016 by ClydeBank Media LLC
Interior Design: Katie Poorman, Copyright © 2016 by ClydeBank Media LLC

ClydeBank Media LLC
P.O Box 6561
Albany, NY 12206
Printed in the United States of America

ISBN-13 : 978-1-945051-05-0

HANDS-ON TRAINING & SUPPORT TO **REACH YOUR GOALS FASTER.**

CLYDEBANK MEDIA
CAMPUS

SELF-PACED ONLINE COURSES TAUGHT BY EXPERT INSTRUCTORS

GROUP DISCUSSION FORUMS

ACCESSIBLE ON ALL DEVICES

LIFETIME ACCESS

MONTHLY COACHING CALLS

CERTIFICATE OF COMPLETION

UPDATED REGULARLY

• INVESTING • INTRINSIC VALUE • PERSONAL FINANCE •
• CREDIT REPAIR • HOME BUYING •

GET ACCESS FOR 70% OFF

www.clydebankmedia.com/investing-campus

contents

BEFORE YOU START READING, DOWNLOAD YOUR FREE DIGITAL ASSETS!

Visit the URL below to access your free Digital Asset files that are included with the purchase of this book.

☑ Summaries   ☑ White Papers

☑ Cheat Sheets   ☑ Charts & Graphs

☑ Articles   ☑ Reference Materials

DOWNLOAD YOURS HERE:

www.clydebankmedia.com/options-assets

introduction

Why This Book Was Written

Hunting for a good beginner-level book on options trading can be a very frustrating endeavor. Many of the books that are labeled "introduction to..." or "...for beginners" are written by high-level brokers or academics who have an annoying habit of talking over their readers' heads and diving headfirst into Wall Street jargon without taking the time to properly explain the basics.

On the flip side, since options trading is such a fertile niche for new ideas, every John Doe and his brother has written a book on options trading, and, unfortunately, an enthusiastic options trader doesn't necessarily make a good writer. Advice from these writers can be not only confusing but also misleading and the results of following said advice can be alarming if not disastrous.

This book, however, was written with the goal of maximizing clarity and readability, all while providing an extensive look at the fundamentals of options trading. You should be more than ready to make your first few trades after reading this book.

| 1 |

Option Basics

Throughout this book, we'll be talking about **stock options**. However, there are other types of options which you may delve into at a later time. Here's a definition of each from the folks at *optionstrading.org*.

- **Stock Options** : The underlying asset for these contracts is shares in a specific publicly listed company.

- **Index Options** : These are very similar to stock options, but rather than the underlying security being stocks in a specific company it is an index – such as the S&P 500.

- **Forex/Currency Options** : Contracts of this type grant the owner the right to buy or sell a specific currency at an agreed rate.

- **Futures Options** : The underlying security for this type is a specified futures contract. A futures option essentially gives the owner the right to enter into that specified futures contract.

- **Commodity Options** : The underlying asset for a contract of this type can be either a physical commodity or a commodity futures contract.

- **Basket Options** : A basket contract is based on the underlying asset of a group of securities which could be made up of stocks, currencies, commodities or other financial instruments.

But let's keep it simple for now. Consider this scenario as a way to understand the basic premise of stock options trading.

I know a fashion designer who is an eccentric genius. She makes incredible dresses that you just can't find anywhere else. There's nothing like them! She makes them all by hand, and she does all the work herself. The only drawback is that she only makes these dresses in the summer, and she only makes about 10 of them each year.

It's the middle of winter, and I've made a deal to buy one of this designer's summer dresses for a price of $100. I've guaranteed the purchase using a contract. The contract states that I have the right to purchase a dress at $100 at any time before the third Friday of September. To secure my option to buy the dress, I paid a fee, or **premium**, of $50.

Note : This $50 is not a deposit or down payment. It will not be deducted from the $100 I will eventually pay to own a dress. The $50 premium is merely the price of my right to buy the dress for $100 before the third Friday in September.

In July, I decide to exercise my option to buy a dress. Per my contract, I pay $100 for the dress. On the same day I decide to go to the designer's Etsy page and take a look at the other dresses she's selling. They are all priced at $200. I decide, rather than keeping the dress, to sell it to another party for $200. Since I paid only $100 plus the premium payment of $50, I profited $50 from my purchase of an option.

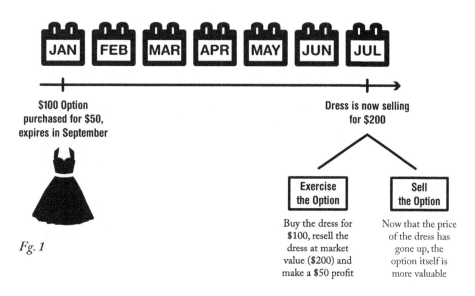

Fg. 1

What are Options?

Options are contracts. They entitle a party to purchase or sell a specific asset (stock, real estate, merchandise) for a specific price within a certain window of time. They also oblige a separate party to sell or purchase the specific asset. For instance, in the example above, just as my option contract guaranteed me the right to buy the dress for $100, the dress maker was obliged to sell the dress for $100. In every option contract there is a buyer and a seller. One party, <u>either the buyer or the seller</u>, has an *obligation* to participate in a particular transaction per the dictates of the options contract. The other party, <u>either the buyer or the seller</u>, has the *option* to participate in a particular transaction per the dictates of the options contract. In the example above, I paid $50 for the *option* to buy a dress for $100 before the third Friday in September. Just because I owned this option does not mean that I was obliged to execute it. I was the **owner** or *buyer* of the option. The dressmaker, who was *obligated* to sell me the dress, was the **writer** or *seller* of the option.

2 Key Parties in a Stock Options Trade

the buyer/owner

 Owns the right to buy a specified quantity of a specified stock within a specified timeline

 Is not obligated to exercise the option

 May sell the option to another party at any time and for any price

the seller/writer

 Writies (theoretically) and sells the contract guaranteeing the buyer the right to purchase a specified quantity of a specified stock within a specified timeline

 Is obligated to sell the specified quantity of the specified stock within the specified timeline should the buyer/owner exercise the option

Fg. 2

What are Stocks?

If you're thinking about delving into the world of options, you're probably already familiar with stocks. But, just as a refresher – a stock is a piece of a company. When a company decides to be a "public" company, it issues shares of stock for purchase by the general public. The more "stocks" or pieces you purchase, the more of the company you own, though, in most cases, unless you own thousands of shares, your piece is pretty small.

Now that you are technically a co-owner of this company, you are awarded a portion of the profits. If the company is performing at its best, your stock goes up in price and you see a profit, usually paid to you in the form of dividends, which are sums of money paid out to investors on a regular basis (usually quarterly). But if the company isn't performing well for one reason or another, you assume a loss. In this case, the dividends you receive are lower or, in some cases, you don't receive any at all.

In order to trade options, you DO NOT need to own stock in the company with which you are trading. However, if you're the writer/ seller of the option, then owning the stock will lessen your risk. These are called "covered" options and we'll talk about them in a later chapter.

Options in the Stock Market

Though option contracts have been around in some form since the days of ancient Greece[1], it wasn't until 1973 that the trading of stock options became formally institutionalized in the *Chicago Board Options Exchange (CBOE)*. Prior to the CBOE, the general public was highly mistrustful of trading stock options. Contracts were difficult to enforce, and even brokers had a difficult time accurately pricing options. The CBOE saw to it that stock option contracts were all standardized and that a clearing corporation was formed (Options Clearing Corporation or OCC) that would be responsible for ensuring that contracts were enforced. There was still a lot of doubt about whether options trading would catch on with the general public, but after a few years in business, the CBOE was buzzing with trading activity. Since that time, options trading has become a persistent facet of major securities exchanges across the globe.

Currently, there are a total of six options exchanges in the United States. They all have excellent websites where new and experienced traders can gather general information about options trading as well as more specific information on the listings they handle. These sites are good tools and should be perused as you begin your options journey.

- American Stock Exchange (AMEX) *www.amex.com*
- Boston Options Exchange (BOX) *www.bostonoptions.com*
- Chicago Board Options Exchange (CBOE) *www.cboe.com*
- International Securities Exchange (ISE) *www.ise.com*
- New York Stock Exchange (NYSE/ARCA) *www.nyse.com*
- Philadelphia Stock Exchange (PHLX) *www.phlx.com*

---

[1] Sincere, Michael. *Understanding Options.* New York: McGraw Hill, 2014. Electronic book.

Now, with six markets, the process of options trading seems complicated right off the bat. However, some key participants in your options trading venture will help you navigate these markets and better understand the entire process.

The Broker

If you already have a stock broker, chances are that he or she can also handle options trading for you. However, some brokers specifically deal in options. As with stocks, you simply instruct them as to what kind of transaction you'd like to carry out, and they do the legwork and charge you a commission to put the trade in motion. You can ask them to buy new contracts, sell contracts you already own, or write new contracts to sell. You can also provide them with certain orders about buying and selling at particular prices. In all, they can manage all aspects of your options portfolio.

As you enter the world of options trading, look for a full-service broker rather than a discount broker. The latter merely takes orders and executes them. The former is more expensive commission-wise but should take the time to meet with you personally and get to know your financial circumstances and investment goals.

Once you feel you are sufficiently experienced in the field of options trading and have become quite hands-on in your trading, you may decide to go with the less-expensive option of a discount broker.

The Market Maker

The market maker isn't a person you'll ever meet or even see. Rather, the term refers to a broker-dealer firm that takes on the risk of holding multiple shares of a particular security so that trading in that security can happen. In other words, the market maker does exactly as the name suggests – provides a market for your options order. They are there to keep the markets running smoothly and to ensure a certain amount of liquidity. To accomplish that, they step in if there are no public orders to match a required trade by maintaining a sizeable and diverse portfolio of options contracts.

For example, suppose you want to buy options contracts for Google, but no one from the general public is selling at the moment. The market maker steps in and sells you those options from its own portfolio.

If not for market makers, there would be far fewer transactions occurring, it might be difficult to buy or sell, and the options available would be severely limited.

The Options Clearing Corporation

The *Options Clearing Corporation (OCC)* is the firm that guarantees that options sellers meet their obligations and complete their transactions. As a clearing house, it literally moves billions of dollars a day, which makes it one of the largest equity derivatives clearing organizations in the world. You won't ever need to contact them, most likely, but it's good to know they're there to make trades run smoothly.

Options Industry Council

This is an investor education partnership formed by the six options exchanges mentioned previously. For those new to the options market, the OIC is a wonderful tool and its website provides a plethora of information about listed stock options. Check it out at *www. optionscentral.com.*

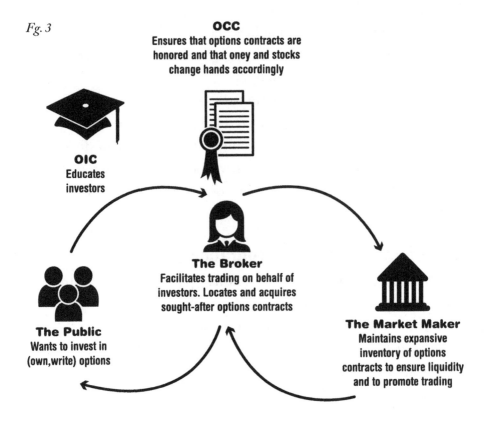

Fg. 3

OCC
Ensures that options contracts are
honored and that oney and stocks
change hands accordingly

OIC
Educates
investors

The Broker
Facilitates trading on behalf of
investors. Locates and acquires
sought-after options contracts

The Public
Wants to invest in
(own,write) options

The Market Maker
Maintains expansive
inventory of options
contracts to ensure liquidity
and to promote trading

Why Were Options Such a Hit?

As you see, options trading has gained a lot of attention over the past few decades. There's no definitive explanation for its resounding success. Just as in any other product or pursuit, there was no way to be sure of that success prior to testing the market. Part of the appeal of options trading, no doubt, is the potential to realize faster and larger profits than in the traditional stock market. Options also provide a way for investors to participate in the stock market with less investment. That's because you don't have to own shares of a stock to trade options associated with that stock. If an investor is familiar with a certain stock and believes she can predict its movement, then purchasing an option allows that investor a chance to capitalize on that stock's behavior without having to purchase the stock outright.

Options vs. Stocks

Not everyone who "plays" the stock market is interested in trading options. Depending on your financial portfolio as well as your goals, your broker may advise against it due to the risk. So whether or not you get involved depends on just how willing you are to take a chance with your cash.

Indeed, the stock market is simpler to navigate than the options market. In general, you only have to worry about one thing – whether the stock is going up or down. With options, as you'll see in future chapters, you have to get three things right – the direction it's moving, the timing, and the magnitude. In stock transactions, losses tend to be smaller – you rarely lose 100% of your investment as you might with options. Furthermore, if a stock is in a losing position, you can usually just wait it out until it gets back to fair market value.

Options can be scary, but they do have their advantages. Investing in options allows you to tie up a lot less of your cash on hand, as you'll see when we discuss strategies in a later chapter. Hence, options have greater leveraging power. The potential for higher returns is certainly present as well, particularly with less cash outlay. Finally, options are a very flexible investment tool and create more investment alternatives, ideal for those who want a diverse portfolio. Of course, neither stocks nor options carry with them any sort of guarantee. It's your job, along with your broker, to determine what kind of risks you are able to take and if you can live with the potential consequences. That's why books like this, which outline the basics and explain the strategies, are essential.

| 2 |

Trading Fundamentals

For the reader who is completely new to the world of options trading, patience is indeed a virtue as you navigate the often confusing world of stock options. Keep the faith that you will eventually gain an understanding of how options work and of how the different types of options and the different strategies come into play. This book makes it as easy as possible for you.

Trading options may appear, at a glance, to be complicated, but it's really not so bad once you grasp some of the fundamental concepts and jargon involved. You may have to reread certain passages of this book again and again and may have to resort to some pencil-and-paper calculations to figure it all out, but with some practice and a little "virtual" trading, you'll eventually be comfortable enough to give it a shot.

This chapter provides you with some proverbial nuts-and-bolts and reviews the two main types of options trading: the put option and the call option.

Calls & Puts—What's in a Name?

Perhaps the easiest type of option to understand is the call option. It's called a *call* because the buyer/owner may "call" for the sale of the stock at any time prior to the expiration date. In the dress example from Chapter 1, I purchased a "call" option on a designer dress and exercised the option by "calling in" my right to make the purchase for $100, even though the same dresses were selling on Etsy for $200.

The person who sells the call, also known as the writer of the call, agrees to sell the stock (**underlying asset**) at the agreed-upon price at any point before the expiration date.

> Note : A quick word about expiration dates in options trading—the writer/seller of the call or put option always specifies an expiration date. Usually this is done just by stating the month, and it is assumed that the option will expire on the third Friday of the expiration month. For example, you can purchase an option contract in March with a May expiration. Unless otherwise specified, the contract will expire on the third Friday of May.

An investor would choose to buy a call when they believe that the underlying asset will see an increase in price over a certain period of time. Calls have an expiration date and, as such, the asset can be purchased at any time prior to or on that date.

Expiration dates are important. In order for the buyer/owner of an option to profit from it, the stock in question must perform in a certain way (it must either go up or down) within a certain period of time. The longer the time period before expiration, the greater chance, theoretically, that the stock will perform in the desired way. Therefore— the most important principle of options trading is—*time is money.* The more time exists in an options contract between the point at which the option is secured and the point at which the option expires, the more valuable the contract will be.

The idea of "time as money," specifically in reference to options trading, is emphasized thoroughly in Edward Olmstead's book *Options for the Beginner and Beyond.* Olmstead says that, "This phrase [time is money] should always be in the back of your mind as you deal with options.[2]"

> Note : Other traders and trading reference publications, such as <u>Options Made Easy</u> by Guy Cohen, have coined the term **time value** to refer to the added value of an option in light of how much time is left before the contract expires[3].

---

[2] Olmstead, Edward. *Options for the Beginner and Beyond.* Upper Saddle River, NJ: FT Prentice Hall. 2006. Print.

[3] Cohen, Guy. *Options Made Easy.* London: FT Prentice Hall, 2005. Print.

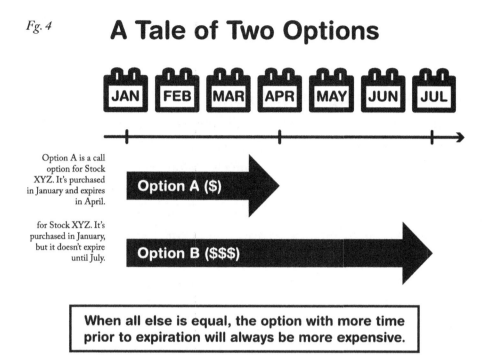

Fg. 4

A Tale of Two Options

Option A is a call option for Stock XYZ. It's purchased in January and expires in April.

for Stock XYZ. It's purchased in January, but it doesn't expire until July.

When all else is equal, the option with more time prior to expiration will always be more expensive.

*Note : It may also be prudent to note here that there are **American-style options** and **European-style options**. This book focuses on American-style options. The difference between the two is that American-style options may be exercised at any point prior to the expiration date, whereas European- style options must be exercised on the expiration date, if at all.*

The opposite of a call option is a *put* option, and, like the call option, a put option has a buyer/owner and a seller/writer. A put option is so named because the owner has the right to "put" his stock back into the market at an agreed-upon price at any time within an agreed-upon time frame. The writer of a put option simply agrees to purchase said stock at the agreed-upon price at any time within the agreed-upon time frame. An investor would buy a put option if they were expecting the underlying asset to fall in price.

So there you have it, the basics of option trading. From these fundamental concepts come literally countless scenarios and opportunities for profitable trading. Let's cultivate your understanding of the dynamics of options trading by going through a few specific examples of each type of trade.

Buying a Call Option on Exxon

Let's say you're about to buy a call option on Exxon Mobil™. Now, before you do so, it's important to understand why you've decided to make this particular move. How much is Exxon Mobil selling for right now? At this very moment, let's say Exxon is selling for $80. Ok, you think the stock is going to go up significantly in the next two months, so you're going to purchase a call option for 100 shares of Exxon Mobile at a *strike price* (see Glossary) of $85, and you're going to set your expiration month for March, two months away. This means that you're buying the right to purchase 100 shares of the stock at $85 at any time between now (January) and the third week in March. The trader jargon for your call option position is: long one XOM Mar 85 call.

Note: Remember, expiration dates are assumed to be the 3rd Friday of the expiration month unless otherwise specified. Also, XOM are the call letters for Exxon Mobile. Don't worry if you don't understand all components of the jargon just yet. That will come in time.

Note: The strike prices and the cost of the options in these examples are fictitious. You can view an up-to-date options schedule by visiting your brokerage's website, or by accessing the websites of the OIC, CBOE, Google, or Yahoo[4]. Here's an example of what a typical option listing (sometimes referred to as an "option chain") looks like on Yahoo Finance. As you can see, you set an $85 strike price for September 1st 2018 (two months away from the time of the query) then the call option can be bought for about a dollar per share[5]. As for the other columns, their importance is discussed later on in this book.

---

[4] Sincere, Michael. *Understanding Options*. New York: McGraw Hill, 2014. Electronic book.
[5] Yahoo Finance. *finance.yahoo.com.* accessed 7/18/2018.

Exxon Mobil Corporation (XOM)
NYSE - Nasdaq Real Time Price. Currency in USD

82.07 -0.24 (-0.29%)
As of 12:57PM EDT. Market open
Calls for September 21, 2018

Contract Name	Last Trade Date	Strike	Last Price	Bid	Ask	Change	% Change	Volume	Open Interest	Implied Volatility
XOM180921C00082500	2018-07-18 11:30AM EDT	82.50	1.86	2.00	2.01	-0.28	-13.08%	240	8,015	15.89%
XOM180921C00085000	2018-07-18 12:37PM EDT	85.00	1.06	1.05	1.06	-0.08	-7.02%	951	11,742	15.70%
XOM180921C00087500	2018-07-18 12:37PM EDT	87.50	0.51	0.51	0.53	-0.07	-12.07%	323	18,916	15.93%

Fg. 5

So, if you're brand new to options trading, then you may be wondering why you're reserving the right to buy Exxon stock at a price ($85 per shar e) that's more expensive than its current value of $80 per share. You're doing this because you're betting that Exxon is going to go up in value by the expiration date (third Friday in March). Let's say you (or your broker) find a writer for this option who's willing to sell it to you for $1 per share (all option contracts are quoted on a per share basis). Since you want a call option on 100 shares, you're going to pay a total of $100 to own this option contract.

From here, there are many possible outcomes:

Scenario 1:   The third Friday of March arrives, and the stock still has yet to climb above $85. Your option is essentially worthless, and you're out $100.

Scenario 2:   It's February and you're midway through your contract. Exxon Mobile has climbed to $90 and you call in your option to buy 100 shares at $85. You've made $500 minus the $100 you paid to own the option—$400 in total profit. Believe it or not, under these circumstances, calling in your option is <u>not</u> likely to be the most profitable move.

Scenario 3:   Again, it's February and you're midway through your contract. Exxon Mobile has climbed to $90 and you decide to _sell_ your option contract to another party. Your option contract now has what's commonly referred to as an intrinsic value.

> Note : _The intrinsic value of the option is derived from the fact that the option guarantees the owner the right to purchase Exxon at $85 per share. Meanwhile, Exxon is selling for $90 per share on the open market. The call option thus has an intrinsic value of $5._

call option strike price – current stock price = intrinsic value

Since your option now has an intrinsic value, it's is more valuable than it was when you first purchased it (when Exxon stock was selling for $80). With an intrinsic value of $5, the same option that you bought for $1 per share is now likely to sell for $6 or $7 per share.

> Note : _The per share price of the option is almost always more than its intrinsic value. Why? Because time is money. The new owner of your call option is going to be betting that the Exxon stock is going to climb even higher before the option expires in March. She's buying not just the right to buy the stock at $85 and reap her immediate $5 profit, but she's also buying the right to wait and see if the stock goes higher, potentially making her $85 call more profitable. Time is money._

intrinsic value + time value = the price of a stock option

So, if you have an option contract worth $6 per share that you bought for $1 a share and you sell it, how much profit do you make? The total cost for optioning the 100 shares was $100. Now you're selling at a total sale price of $600. Your profit is an even $500. Compare this to the $400 in total profit you'd have ended up with had you called in the stock per scenario 2.

Scenario 4:   Let's say, again, that it's mid-February. Exxon hasn't climbed in value but instead hovered around the $80 mark. Perhaps some new factor has led you to believe that it's unlikely that the stock is going to climb higher than $85 as you'd originally expected. You can always sell your call option, as is, even though it has no intrinsic value and won't be worth as much as you paid for it now that half the contract time has passed. Nonetheless, it is feasible that you could cut your losses some, perhaps by finding a buyer who will purchase the call option for 50 cents per share. You'd get $50 for your option contract after paying $100, and you'd take a 50% loss.

Selling a Call Option on Disney™

Let's take a look at a possible scenario in which you want to sell or write a call option. When you write a call option you're guaranteeing another party the purchase of a particular stock at a particular price at particular point in time. You're not required to own the stock in order to write a call option for that stock. This is known as *naked call writing*, and it's quite risky.

Let's say that you own stock in Disney and you want to write a call option contract for 100 shares of the stock. Since you own Disney stock, this is known as covered call writing. Disney is currently trading at $110 per share. However, after years of holding the stock, you're not very optimistic about Disney's acquisition of the YouTube content creation company Makers Studio. On top of that you know their current CEO is looking to retire by the end of the quarter, and you're not thrilled about his replacement prospects. You're looking to lighten your load on Disney. Selling/writing a call option for the stock can help you both get rid of Disney and possibly make some extra money in the meantime.

It's June and you write a call option with a $120 strike price and an expiration month of November. The position is technically called:

short one DIS nov 120 call. DIS is the ticker symbol for Disney. Because you're giving the owner/buyer of the call option over four months Jun-Nov to wait for the Disney stock to climb, your option may sell at a nice high price. Let's say you're able to sell the option at $5 per share or $500 total. You immediately receive the $500 but are obliged to sell 100 shares of Disney at $120 per share at any time before the third Friday in November.

Fg. 6

Decoding the Jargon

Simply refers to the number of options contracts being bought or sold. "One" contract = 100 shares worth, "Two" contracts = 200 shares, and so on.

The expiration month. In this example the expiration date, by default, would be the third Friday of the month unless specified elsewhere.

The type of option being bought or sold, a "call" or a "put."

Short one DIS nov 120 call

In general market lingo, a "long" position entails owning and a "short" position entails owing. In options trading the writer of the call or put option *owes* the owner the right to exercise the specified option. Therefore the writer/seller's position is always "short" and the owner/buyer's position is always "long."

The call letters of the stock being optioned.

The strike price for the option.

Scenario 1:   The stock stays below $120 and, naturally, no one ever calls it in. No one is going to voluntarily purchase 100 Disney shares at $120 when they could buy it for less. You've already made $500 by selling the option and you're free to write another call option if you're still looking to dump Disney in the most profitable way.

Scenario 2:   It's October, the trailer for the next Star Wars installment is released, and it looks a whole lot better than anyone had anticipated. Suddenly you're not so sure that you want to get rid of your Disney stock. The stock is trading at $122, two dollars above the strike price, and it may be destined to go even higher. The call option you wrote already has an intrinsic value of $2 and will probably sell for more than that, a lot more considering that the option sold for $5 per share with no intrinsic value at all. But then again, you also have to consider that there's less time left in the contract. It's due to expire on the third Friday of November. Let's say that the call option that you sold can now be rebought for $8 a share. Since it's $3 more expensive per share than what you sold it for originally, if you decide to buy it back (because you don't want to be forced to sell your Disney stock), it's going to cost $800, giving you a net loss of $300. But, if Disney keeps climbing, you'll end up better than you would have had you sold the stock at the end of the call contract.

Note : Even if the stock goes above $120 early in the contract, you will likely never have the stock called away until the November expiration date is very close. Why? Because if the stock jumps up fast and early, then not only is your option likely to have more intrinsic value, but there's also going to be plenty of time left on the contract (time value). These two factors will make the call option spike in price, and the current owner of the option will stand to realize more profit through selling the option than by calling it in. Ultimately though, if the price is climbing, someone will eventually call away your stock before the expiration date. On the flip side, if the stock does not increase in value-- let's say it drops to $105--- then, of course, no one is going to buy the stock at the $120 call price. You'll have simply made $500 by selling the call option, and, if you want, you can turn around and write another call option contract. This is a good approach to use if you ultimately do want to part ways with it.

Scenario 3:   Let's say that you were right about the whole succession issue with Disney. They're not going to be able to assure their investors that they've got the right leadership in place for the next generation. Two months into the call contract, the price of Disney falls to $100 a share. It doesn't seem likely that the $120 call option that you sold is ever going to be exercised, and, meanwhile, the value of that option has decreased tremendously since the current price of the stock is lower and there's only half as much time left on the contract. At this point, if you want to, you can buy back the call option for pennies on the dollar and turn a quick profit. You should only do this, though, if you believe that there's still a chance that the stock may rebound back up to $120, at which point you can either sell it again, or do nothing and just keep your stock.

There's really no limit to the scenarios and possibilities. When dealing with options, there are always a lot of options.

Buying a Put Option on General Electric™

Remember, buying a put option is buying the right to put your shares back on the market at a certain price—the strike price—within a given period of time. Usually, put options are bought when the purchaser believes that a stock he already owns is destined to decline in value, and he's willing to pay money to guarantee that he has the right to sell the stock at the strike price for a certain period of time.

It's April and you've got some GE stock worth $29 a share. You come across some information that could be either good news or bad news for GE, you're not sure which. You don't want to sell off your stock, but you don't want to lose your shirt, so you decide to buy a put option that guarantees your right to unload 100 shares of GE at $30 per share. The contract expiration month is June, so your position is named: *Long one GE Jun 30 put.* The stock currently sells for $29 per share, but you bought the put option at $3 per share, so the $1 per share you would have gained from selling immediately (the intrinsic value) is offset by the price of the option.

*Note : You don't even have to own GE or any stock to buy a put option. Buying a put option without owning the stock is known as buying a **naked put**. If the stock goes down as you anticipated, you'll usually be able to resell the put option at a higher price. In other words, when GE was trading at $29 you paid $300 ($3 per share) to own a contract, which entitles you to sell 100 shares of GE at $30 per share. That put option is going to be a heck of a lot more valuable than $300 if GE plunges to $27 per share, assuming there's still some time left on the contract, as the buyer purchasing the put option will be paying a little more than the intrinsic value in hopes that the stock will continue its decline in value. If the buyer, for instance, is willing to pay $4 per share for the put option, then you will net a profit of $100. It won't matter whether or not you actually ever owned the stock or not, all you did was buy (and then sell) an option to put that particular stock in the hands of a buyer for $30 per share.*

In the event that the stock never falls as expected but remains at $29 and the contract is near expiration, the price of the option will fall closer and closer to its intrinsic value of $1, at which point you can sell it off for $100 and take a $200 loss. Again, you don't necessarily have to have possession of any real GE stock to execute these transactions.

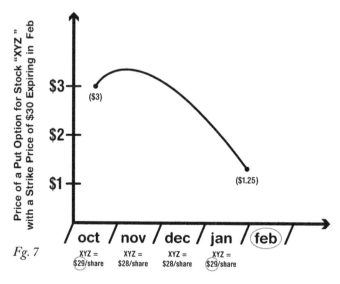

Fg. 7

Fg. 7 : Even though the intrinsic value of the option is the same in October and January ($1), the value of the option is significantly less in January because it has less time value (less time remaining before it expires in February). As options approach their expiration dates, their prices get closer and closer to their intrinsic values.

Selling a Put Option on McDonalds™

In this example, we're going to switch things up by envisioning the sale of a put option within the context of a short sell. Short selling is when you bet against the performance of a particular stock or group of stocks. The practice of short selling garnered much attention in the aftermath of the 2008 financial crisis in the United States. Here's how it works:

Let's say McDonald's is currently selling for $120 per share, but you think that the fact that they started selling breakfast all day is ultimately going to dip into their profit margins and the value of the stock will soon go down. You're betting against McDonald's.

So you borrow – yes, borrow – 100 shares of McDonald's. Your broker is going to charge you a hefty fee for this transaction, so be sure you know what you're doing. When you borrow shares, what you are doing is temporarily controlling shares in a certain company with an agreement to return the stock at a certain time. So someone out there who owns 100 shares of McDonald's stock has allowed you to take those 100 shares temporarily on the sole condition that you agree to return the 100 shares of McDonald's to the original owner after, let's say, two months.

Once you have the McDonald's stock, you can, of course, do whatever you want with it. If you were to short the stock, then you would immediately sell it all at its current price of $120 per share. You would now have $12,000 in cash. If you were correct and McDonald's takes a dip to, let's say to $110 per share, then you would simply buy back the 100 shares of McDonald's stock for $11,000 and you would then have the 100 shares of McDonald's ready to return to the lender. You would have made $1,000 on your short sell minus any fees you paid to borrow the stock. Assuming you weren't charged over $1,000, it was a profitable short sell.

Now, here's where selling a put option may be a wise move. Let's say that midway through your short selling of McDonald's stock, they release a new breakfast item, a high protein McMuffin or some other gimmick that you think is going to be successful and ultimately prevent McDonald's stock from dropping as low as you'd originally thought. Let's say the stock is trading at $110, you still have some time before you have to return the 100 McDonald's shares to lender, and because of this new item, you don't think the stock is going to drop much lower. So you decide to sell a put option at $105, whereby you agree to buy 100 shares of McDonald's stock at $105 per share by the time your contract expires, let's say, by August. To put it into jargon your position is: *short one Aug 105 put.* Let's say the put option sells for $6 per share. You immediately have $600 in cash just for selling the option, but you have the obligation to buy 100 shares of McDonald's stock for $105 per share at a future date; these same 100 shares will eventually be returned to the party from whom you borrowed the stock. So if you're wrong about the Protein McMuffin and it turns out to be a big flop and drives the price down to $95 a share, then you're going to be forced to buy back your 100 shares at the above-market price of $105, because you sold the put option. Nonetheless, since, in this scenario, you originally shorted the stock at $120, you'll still likely make a profit at the end of the day.

On the flip side, if you were correct and the Protein McMuffin stabilized the McDonald's stock and it didn't drop too far below $105, then you've made an extra $600 in profit by selling the put option. How? Simple, you still buy back 100 shares of McDonald's at $105 (a total price of $10,500), which is $1,500 less than its value when you first borrowed and sold it ($12,000), plus you've got your $600 in profit for selling the put option, a total profit of $2,100 minus any brokerage and other fees paid for borrowing the stock and for selling the put option.

Ultimately, in the McDonald's scenario, there is profitability in both of the considered outcomes, but only because it assumes that the short sell was successful. The only question became whether selling the put option would add to or detract from the profit gained on the assumedly successful short sell. As a player of the market, you should know that the short sell itself is incredibly risky, as once you sell off the shares after you borrow them, the price could skyrocket, forcing you to buy back the shares you borrowed with infinite loss potential. Be careful.

At this point you should have a basic grasp of the mechanics, terminologies, strategies, and risk factors involved in options trading. If you feel totally lost, then read through this chapter again before moving on. As Jimmy Cliff says, "You can get it if you really want."

| 3 |

A Sound Strategy for a Beginner

One of the fundamental challenges of teaching options trading to beginners is that there are many pitfalls, and if you just go into the market guns blazing, you will likely come up short. Many gurus and authors have thus turned their attentions to the search for good, simple, conservative trading strategies for beginner-level traders. Ideally, you will use these simple strategies to get a feel for options trading and to steadily learn more and more about the details, metrics, and more complex strategies that may come into play if you continue to trade.

Selling the Covered Call

Several authors and experts, among them Michael Sincere, author of *Understanding Options*, has argued that the selling of the ***covered call*** is one of the best ways to christen your options trading journey[6]. Similar sentiment has been echoed by *stocktrader.com* in their published list of *6 Great Options Strategies for Beginners*. The covered call is at the top of their list[7]. It is the opinion of this author that the gurus aren't promoting covered calls for beginners because they represent a somehow uniquely simple form of options trading, but instead, because they are a highly palatable way of introducing options into your general trading affairs.

Here's why: as you may recall from Chapter 2, when you sell a call (any call), you're guaranteeing another party the right to purchase a

---

[6] Sincere, Michael. *Understanding Options*. New York: McGraw Hill, 2014. Electronic book.

[7] Wolfinger, Mark. *6 Great Options Strategies for Beginners*. March 27, 2009. StockTrader.Com. Date accessed: 12/16/15

stock at an agreed-upon price –the strike price—before an agreed-upon period of time has expired. What makes the sale of the call "covered" is your ownership of the stock—known as the "underlying asset"—for which you are selling the call. In the example in Chapter 2, you sold a call option for Disney stock, and you did so because you owned Disney and *selling your Disney Stock was already part of your larger strategy.*

For options beginners, get your feet wet by choosing a stock that you already own (100 shares, preferably) and are looking to unload. Hence, a covered call can provide you an opportunity to make some money before you eventually sell off the stock. In the fictitious Disney example from Chapter 2, you sold a covered call option for 100 shares of Disney at a $120 strike price—*short one DIS Nov 120 call*—for $5 per share, a grand total of $500. Now, for the first-time options trader, the worst case scenario is that the price of Disney skyrockets and you miss out on a big return from the normal sale of the stock, as you're forced to sell it off at $120 per share to the owner of the call. That said, you're already going into the transaction with an intention to unload the Disney stock at a price that you, at least at the time, think is reasonable. Therefore, if you stick to covered calls for your first several option trades, you'll be able to directly set limits for your losses, meanwhile, you'll learn more about options trading and will be able to more comfortably integrate options into your overall investment strategy.

Ideally, selling covered calls on stocks you want to sell anyway will culminate in a cash influx. When you sell a covered call you will, of course, get paid for it. This payment is known as a "premium." In the Disney example, the premium for selling the call option was $500. If the option is never exercised, then the seller pockets the premium, keeps the stock, and is free to put another covered call out onto the market and pocket another premium. This can be a great way to keep your stocks generating income for you, even as you're preparing to part ways with them.

Dumping MGM

Let's say you're brand new to options and ready to sell your MGM™ Stock (MGM). Meanwhile, you'd like to make some money on your way out of the stock and maybe try your hand at options trading. Let's first take a look at the *options chain*:

MGM Resorts International (MGM)
NYSE - Nasdaq Real Time Price. Currency in USD

31.02 -0.22 (-0.70%)
As of 3:59PM EDT. Market open

December 21, 2018 ▼ │ In The Money

Calls for December 21, 2018

Contract Name	Last Trade Date	Strike	Last Price	Bid	Ask	Change	% Change	Volume	Open Interest	Implied Volatility
MGM181221C00031000	2018-07-18 1:06PM EDT	31.00	2.45	2.46	2.54	-0.23	-8.58%	3	5,351	31.32%
MGM181221C00035000	2018-07-18 9:43AM EDT	35.00	1.04	0.96	1.00	-0.05	-4.59%	2	5,486	29.10%

Fg. 8

As you can see, there's a drop down menu below the quoted price that allows you to select an expiration date for your call option. We are accessing the options chain on July 18, 2018 and have pulled up available contracts with an expiration date of December 15, 2016, about five months away. Our objective is to sell a call option contract (100 shares) for our MGM shares. How do you use information found in the option chain to determine your sale price?

If you don't already know what **bid prices** and **ask prices** are, then it's definitely time to learn. These prices determine how much it's going to cost to buy or sell your options. Since you're selling, the bid price for a particular option represents what's immediately available to you. Look at the table in *Fg. 8*. Specifically take a look at the option contract with the $35 strike price. As you can see, there's an ask price of $1.00 and a bid price of $.96. This means that some party is prepared to immediately pay 96 cents per share to own this call option contract. There is also a party willing to sell this call option for $1.00 per share. What does this tell you? Well, for starters, if you want to guarantee your sale of the call option, then you can do so by accepting the bid price of $.96 and selling your covered call (100 shares worth) for a total of $96. Seems a little skimpy, huh? If you're just starting in options trading, and especially if you're looking at smaller spreads (the difference between the bid and the ask prices), then you may want to go ahead and sell your covered call at the bid price to ensure that you're trade is filled. If you're already familiar with exploiting the wiggle room between bids and ask prices, then you may want to jump right in with a **limit order**, in which you agree to purchase a certain financial asset (stocks, options, etc.) at or below a certain price. For example, you could instruct your broker to "sell one April December MGM at $.98 or better.[8]" If you've been wondering, what the "one" means in option lingo, it refers to the buying or selling of "one" options contract (100 shares). If you *sell two December MGM call at $.98 or better*, then you're selling two contracts (200 shares), and you'll be paid $196 for the trade rather than $98, assuming your limit order is filled at $.98 per share.

If you're still having trouble getting your head around the concept of asks and bids, then imagine your brokerage as an import business, like Pier 1, that ships all of its products from South East Asia. There's a particular cost to the business for each product because of the transportation expense and the cost of manufacturing the product. There's also a particular retail price. The import business owner is not going to want to sell you one of her products at cost, because she won't make any profit whatsoever. She'd prefer that you just pay retail price, but that doesn't mean that she'd be unwilling to unload the product if you were interested in paying somewhere between the product cost and the retail price. Bottom line, flexibility is available, but there's no guarantee that your negotiations will be fruitful.

---

[8] Fontanills, George A. *The Options Course, Second Edition. High Profit and Low Stress Trading Methods.* Hoboken, NJ. John Wiley & Sons Inc. 2005. Print.

In the Money (ITM) or Out of the Money (OTM)

Notice in your attempts to sell your covered call for MGM that you're paying particular attention to the bottom most call contract, the one with the strike price of $35. The other contract (with the strike price of $30) has a little blue marker that denotes it as being *In the Money (ITM)*. If an option is ITM, it means that exercising the option immediately will yield a profit. That is, of course, if you don't take into account the cost of acquiring the option to begin with.

In *Fg. 8* the topmost call contract is ITM and the bottom most, the one you're looking at with the strike price of $35, is OTM. The $30 MGM call contract has a strike price ($30), which is less than the value of the stock. Therefore, if the owner of said option immediately called in the stock at $30, she'd be making a profit of $.02 per share. That said, a price was paid to obtain the option. If that price was more than $.02 per share, then there was actually no net profit made, even though the call option was ITM. Therefore, if an option is ITM, it's going to increase in price, and if the option is OTM, then the option will lower in price. Now, it's important to understand that the parameters of OTM and ITM change with the type of option being considered. Let's take a look at the put options on the market for December 21st for MGM. See *Fg.9* below.

| Puts for December 21, 2018 | | | | | | | | | | |
Contract Name	Last Trade Date	Strike	Last Price	Bid	Ask	Change	% Change	Volume	Open Interest	Implied Volatility
MGM181221P00029000	2018-07-17 3:57PM EDT	29.00	1.39	1.39	1.46	0.00	-	150	2,377	29.69%
MGM181221P00030000	2018-07-13 1:24PM EDT	30.00	1.96	1.79	1.86	+1.96	+100.00%	19	310	29.22%
MGM181221P00031000	2018-07-12 1:53PM EDT	31.00	2.61	2.23	2.33	+2.61	+100.00%	1	1,192	26.81%
MGM181221P00032000	2018-07-17 11:54AM EDT	32.00	2.77	2.73	2.82	0.00	-	10	284	27.81%

Fg. 9

Notice that the baby blue "ITM" highlight is used to denote the put option with the strike price of $32. This is because for put options, which represent a guaranteed right to "put" or sell stock back to the market, the strike price must be higher than the stock value in order for a profit to be realized. In *Fg. 9*, the put option that's ITM has a strike price of $32 and a bid-ask spread of $2.73-$2.82. The per share profit realized from immediately exercising this put option is $.98 ($32-$31.02), which, of course, is offset by the price of purchasing the option. In order for any option (ITM or OTM) to be truly profitable for a buyer, the stock price (and/or the option price) must always move in the right direction within the allotted time. In other words, the direct profit obtained by calling in the stock or putting it on the market must be greater than the price you paid to obtain the option.

> *Note : When the current price of the stock is the same as the strike price, then the option is considered to be "At the Money." It is common for an option to be referred to as "At the Money" even if it's off by a few cents up or down. Also, in his book, Understanding Options, Michael Sincere points out an important rule of thumb for traders—don't ever make the mistake of confusing an option's being ITM for its profitability. As was already explained in this section, ITM and OTM don't in and of themselves have an influence on net profitability. The only thing these terms explain is the relationship between the stock price and the option's strike price[9].*

Stock XYZ is currently priced at $150 per share

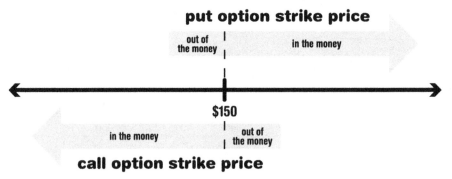

Fg. 10

---

[9] Sincere, Michael. *Understanding Options.* New York: McGraw Hill, 2014. Electronic book.

When you're just starting out with options trading and selling a covered call, it's better if you choose a contract with a strike price that's slightly out of the money. Your thinking should be something akin to the following: 'I've got 100 shares of DKT, currently valued at $32.18, that I'm looking to unload. I'd be happy to sell it off at $35 a share, so I'm going to let the stock work for me in the meantime—I'm going to sell a call option with a $35 strike price. I'll make some money in the short term, and I'll only have to sell my stock if it goes up to $35 or higher by the end of the expiration period. If the call option expires without ever being redeemed, then I'll just issue a new one and continue to generate more money from the premiums received. I'll keep track of how much money my stock has generated, as this is going to lower my *cost basis* for the stock, and ideally, make my overall involvement with DFT a more profitable and successful endeavor.'

Disclaimer

Keep in mind that when we advocate selling the covered call option as a conservative play for a beginner, we're doing so because the strategy is easy to understand and can be easily fit into a greater investment strategy. We're not implying that this strategy is more likely than others to turn a profit or minimize risk. In his book, Options for the Beginner and Beyond, author and trader, Edward Olmstead, provides a reality check for the covered call trade strategy and issues the following caveats:

- Olmstead advises monitoring the value of the underlying asset, the stock, more closely than the value of the option. Just because you've sold a covered option on the stock does not oblige you to keep it if it falls too low[10].

---

[10] Olmstead, Edward. *Options for the Beginner and Beyond.* Upper Saddle River, NJ: FT Prentice Hall. 2006. Print.

> *Note : Olmstead makes a good point, and it's especially relevant for beginner-level options traders. If you're the owner of 100 shares of a stock, even if you want to sell it, and are using the stock to sell covered call options, then you're still likely to be more affected overall by the performance of the stock rather than by the performance of the option, even during the time in which the option is active. Don't let your covered call options distract you from your big-picture strategy.*

- Olmstead also warns against getting too greedy and impulsively buying back your call option in the event that the stock shoots up, "Avoid buying back the option for a loss unless you have a good reason to do so." If the stock goes up, you still made a profit. Maybe it's not as large as it might have been had you not sold the option, but it's still a net profit in your overall investment strategy. Be happy with it and move on[11].

Avoid These Beginner Mistakes

Everyone makes mistakes with their investments, whether you're trading stocks and options, buying gold and silver, or purchasing real estate. A good pre-investing education, can help you avoid some of the common pitfalls that claim beginning options investors and send them running for the hills.

Consider these:

Plan to work & work your plan

You should always enter options deals with a plan, most specifically an exit plan. Many of us make a definitive exit plan only to get caught up in the moment and change it. Choose your upside and downside exit points in advance and adhere to those decisions. Don't wait around because you think a stock is going to soar through the

---

[11] Sincere, Michael. *Understanding Options.* New York: McGraw Hill, 2014. Electronic book.

roof and you'll make even more. The converse is true as well. Don't ditch your exit strategy in hopes that a stock will come up and you'll recoup more of your losses. It's easy to let your emotions get the best of you during trading, especially with your money at risk, but you need to put those emotions aside as best you can. That doesn't mean, of course, that you can't reassess your plan at all. You just don't want to do it in the middle of a trade.

Don't buy it because it's cheap

Do you know someone who heads to the supermarket with stacks of coupons, buying everything with these cents-off offers whether they need the items or not? Well, some traders operate that way, too. Brokers warn new options traders about the temptation to buy deeply out-of-the-money options just because they're cheap. This is especially true of those working with limited funds. If an option is very far out-of-the-money, it has a long way to move before it becomes profitable. Hence, it's often a better idea to start with options that cost more and are more in-the-money and have an expiration date that's further out. Ultimately, the reward may not be as large, but the risk will certainly be lower.

Remember that losses are a fact of life

You can't avoid losses altogether when you're dealing with options trading, so don't fear losses. Losses happen, but you just need to learn how to keep them as small as possible. Inevitably you'll suffer a few sizeable ones as well, but you can't let that scare you away from the market. Don't just think about your trades in the context of whether or not they make money for your portfolio, but think of whether they are in line with your own rules for trading. That in itself constitutes success. Then accept the fact that you can't control the market.

Be disciplined in your trading

Think about these things before you make any trade: 1) What is a reasonable amount of money for this trade? 2) What entry and exit signals do I need to identify? 3) What is the maximum risk I'm willing to assume for this trade? and 4) Why is it important for me to execute each order according to plan? (See Plan to Work and Work Your Plan.) These are all part of being a disciplined options trader. Discipline also occurs as a result of researching each trade before you take the plunge. In short, you must learn all the things you need to do to trade successfully. You're reading this book, so you're off to a good start!

Practice Makes Perfect

As you learn the particulars of puts and calls, ITM, OTM, and everything else associated with the options trading world, you might want to create a virtual portfolio. Many beginning investors do this with stocks, and it tends to work well with options, too. Anything that makes you feel more comfortable before you put your money on the line is a good thing, and with virtual or "paper" trading, you are free to make mistakes and learn from them.

Paper trading allows you to ready yourself for the tasks involved in options trading. You'll learn to analyze the options available and organize your record keeping, and you'll observe how the market responds to certain factors and how you should respond. You'll be forced to face certain situations that could be nail-biting if your money were truly on the line, but if you do it on paper and succeed, you'll be more confident when it's the real thing.

Some experts discourage paper trading because they believe it's just too easy on the psyche. Options trading can be a true roller coaster ride, and by taking the ride on paper without a true risk, you cannot prepare yourself emotionally for the losses you might encounter as you trade.

Others note that paper trading does not help with the understanding of trade execution.

All of that said, however, if you want to practice first, you can paper trade "on paper" or even do it electronically. The CBOE, for example, offers a free virtual trade tool on its website (*www.cboe.org*), which allows you to test a new strategy before putting it into action. Use their detailed virtual trade screens to get a feel for real options trading. They even offer live chat support when you need it. It's a win-win situation for anyone who's not quite ready to start trading with her investment funds.

If you do this, it's important to create realistic scenarios as you trade. If you're not going to be investing $3 million, then don't paper trade with $3 million! Only use amounts that you're going to be able to afford when it's time to do the real thing. Similarly, don't make aggressive moves that you wouldn't make if this were your actual money. The more you relate your paper trading strategies to YOUR reality, the better you'll do after you exit the virtual world.

Several investment firms offer virtual trading sites, others do not. A few of the better paper trading sites are listed below. Each is a little different and some have limits as to what you can virtually invest. In most cases, you need to open an account (fill out a registration form) to use them.

- *www.thinkorswim.com* – Operated by TD Ameritrade
- *www.optionsxpress.com* – Operated by Charles Schwab
- *www.tradestation.com*
- *www.optionshouse.com*

| 4 |

Key Influencers on Options Prices

The price of a given option at any point in time is influenced by several factors. In this chapter, you'll learn about the most important factors that affect how much you will pay for an option (or how much you will receive for selling one).

Why You Should Care About How Options Are Priced

You may be thinking that options trading is essentially a bet that a stock is going to either rise or decrease in value, which will in turn make a given option valuable or worthless. Why should you care about other factors?

While the price of the underlying asset (the stock) is certainly a huge factor in determining the value of an option, it's most assuredly not the only one. Remember, most of the options you end up owning you will resell, not execute. The goal is essentially the same as it is with any other portfolio strategy: you want to buy low and sell high, and in order to carry out this strategy intelligently, you need to know all of the intricacies that go into determining the price for a given option.

Note : Take a look at some of the extremely cheap, nearly worthless call options for Ford Motor Co. in Fg. 11. In all likelihood, anyone buying an option so far out of the money and with only one month until expiration doesn't truly believe that the stock is going to climb up by $10. They are most likely hoping that the stock climbs up by a modest amount, maybe $3, and that their long-shot call option can be sold back into the market for slightly more than what they paid for it. This is the right way to think about options, as buyable and sellable commodities that are different from stocks only insofar as they come with an expiration date.

45

Ford Motor Company (F)
NYSE - NYSE Delayed Price. Currency in USD

10.87 +0.01 (+0.09%)
At close: 4:02PM EDT

Calls for January 18, 2019

Contract Name	Last Trade Date	Strike	Last Price	Bid	Ask	Change	% Change	Volume	Open Interest	Implied Volatility
F190118C00019870	2018-07-09 11:18AM EDT	19.87	0.01	0.00	0.03	+0.01	+100.00%	31	18,896	41.02%
F190118C00020000	2018-01-26 4:03PM EDT	20.00	0.02	0.02	0.04	-0.01	-33.33%	5	17,634	43.36%
F190118C00021870	2018-07-02 12:01PM EDT	21.87	0.01	0.00	0.01	+0.01	+100.00%	0	11,932	39.84%

Fg. 11

Perhaps George Fontanills puts it best, "The primary reason [for understanding the key influencers of options pricing] is that understanding the key price influences is the simplest method to establish realistic expectations for how an option position is likely to behave under a variety of conditions.[12]"

The Moneyness Factor

Chapter 3 talked about the concept of being in the money (ITM) or *out of the money (OTM)*. The difference between an option's set strike price and the price of the underlying asset or stock is known as the *moneyness* factor, and Fontanills argues that moneyness is the most critical determinant of an option's price. You can see the moneyness factor at work in virtually any option chain. Take, for instance, an option chain for Nielsen Holdings.

In *Fg. 12* a series of call options are listed for Nielsen Holdings (NLSN), complete with the current bid and ask prices. The per share price of NLSN is $30.76, and the strike prices for the call options range from $26 to $34. Since these are call options, any strike price below the current price is said to be ITM. As you are sure to see in most any option chain, options become less expensive the less in the money and the more out of the money they become.

---

[12] Fontanills, George A. *The Options Course, Second Edition. High Profit and Low Stress Trading Methods.* Hoboken, NJ. John Wiley & Sons Inc. 2005. Print.

Nielsen Holdings plc (NLSN)
NYSE - NYSE Delayed Price. Currency in USD

30.76 +0.11 (+0.36%)

Calls for July 20, 2018

Contract Name	Last Trade Date	Strike	Last Price	Bid	Ask	Change	% Change	Volume	Open Interest	Implied Volatility
NLSN180720C00026000	1969-12-31 8:00PM EDT	26.00	3.90	5.10	5.40	+3.90	+100.00%	0	0	200.20%
NLSN180720C00028000	2018-06-22 9:43AM EDT	28.00	3.70	3.10	3.30	+3.70	+100.00%	0	2	133.01%
NLSN180720C00029000	2018-06-29 9:57AM EDT	29.00	2.17	2.10	2.30	+2.17	+100.00%	3	11	102.15%
NLSN180720C00030000	2018-07-03 9:57AM EDT	30.00	1.00	1.10	1.30	+1.00	+100.00%	2	16	69.14%
NLSN180720C00031000	2018-07-17 11:06AM EDT	31.00	0.11	0.10	0.15	0.00	-	8	76	22.66%
NLSN180720C00032000	2018-07-16 3:58PM EDT	32.00	0.05	0.00	0.05	+0.05	+50.00%	36	783	34.77%
NLSN180720C00033000	2018-07-10 3:57PM EDT	33.00	0.10	0.00	0.05	+0.10	+100.00%	2	183	53.13%
NLSN180720C00034000	1969-12-31 8:00PM EDT	34.00	0.11	0.00	0.05	+0.11	+100.00%	0	24	60.94%

Fg. 12

Note: Fg. 12 features call options. For put options, the strike price must be higher than the underlying asset price to be considered ITM.

Time Value & Time Decay

The second most critical factor that influences an option's price is the time of expiration on the contract. As was stated in Chapter 2 and emphasized continually by writer and trader, Edward Olmstead, "time is money." The time factor is also the most important distinction between owning a stock and owning an option. Because options lose their value over time, they are considered *wasting assets*. The phenomenon of an option losing value over time is commonly referred to as *time decay*.

In Olmstead's book, *Options for the Beginner and Beyond*, he offers a really interesting way to think about time value – in terms of hype. Olmstead compares the expensive option contract with lots of time left until expiration to a hot, flash-in-the-pan Christmas toy whose hype drives its price up, but only on a temporary basis. Also, rather than "moneyness," Olmstead uses the term *intrinsic value* and his explanation of time value (or hyped value) in relation to intrinsic value is quite useful. He suggests that the hyped value of an option can be seen clearly as what's left over after the option's intrinsic value has been taken into account[13].

---

[13] Olmstead, Edward. *Options for the Beginner and Beyond.* Upper Saddle River, NJ: FT Prentice Hall. 2006. Print.

Let's take Olmstead's theory and apply it to a specific case study. For instance, let's say you've got 100 shares of Alphabet Inc. valued at $758.09 per share (GOOG), which is going to cost you about $75,809. You can buy a call option with a $750 strike price for about $10.60 per share. This option is in the money (ITM), and its intrinsic value can be calculated by subtracting the strike price ($750) from the price of the asset itself ($758.09), which leaves you with $8.09 for the intrinsic value. That's about $2.50 less than the price of the option. Therefore, as Holmstead might say, the leftover $2.50 is the "hyped value" or time value of the option. As it turns out, you're looking at a call option that expires in only 3 days, so that explains the relatively small hype value/time value.

Let's look at that same option, but with a more substantial duration remaining on the contract. Let's do a contract of five weeks rather than three days and see what happens. It turns out that the same option is now going to cost you $26 per share. The intrinsic value hasn't changed, it's still $8.09 or ($758.09-$750), but that's because you're looking at an option with 5 weeks (35 days) left in the contract, as opposed to 3 days. Subtracting the intrinsic value of $8.09 from the price of the new option, $26, leaves you with $17.91 in "hyped value."

Note: It may be interesting to note that the 35-day hyped value for the option is only 7.2 times greater than the 3-day hyped value, even though 35 days is 11.7 times longer than 3 days.

Note: It may also be interesting to note that only stocks that are ITM are said to have intrinsic value. Therefore, if you're considering purchasing an option that's not in the money, you can rest assured that the bulk of what you're paying for is considered "time value.[14]*"*

Now let's take that last example in which you calculated a time value/hype value of $17.91 and take a look at the put option for the same

---

[14] Vine, Simon. Options: Trading Strategy and Risk Management. Hoboken, NJ. John Wiley & Sons Inc. 2005. Print

stock (GOOG) at the same strike price ($750) and for the same 35-day period. It's no accident that you find that put option priced at $17.87, essentially the same price as the time value of the call option. This is no coincidence. The reasons are rather complicated and perhaps beyond the scope of this beginner-level text, but what's important to accept is that time value/hype value should always be consistent between calls and puts when you're dealing with both the same underlying asset and the same strike price.

Note: For the put option discussed above, the $17.87 price is entirely driven by time value, as the option has no intrinsic value. $750 is lower than the price of the asset, therefore the put option, unlike the call option, is out of the money.

Volatility

Volatility refers to the propensity of a certain financial instrument to significantly fluctuate in value over time.

When you think rationally about what makes an option profitable, you will come to the conclusion that there must always be some significant movement in the price of the option, driven by movement in the price of the underlying asset that outpaces the time-decay, which devalues the option. Therefore, if you purchase an option that's not inclined to fluctuate much in price, then there's a much slimmer chance that your option will end up big in the money. On the other hand, if your option is volatile and subject to wide swings in pricing, then you've got a chance to make a big profit.

The way volatility is evaluated and used in trading options is one of the key distinctions between trading in options and trading in conventional stocks. With a conventional stock, high volatility means that not only can you profit big, but you can also lose big. When you own an option, it's either going to be exercised or it's not. If things go really badly and the numbers move against your option with extreme prejudice, the end result is that the option will expire without ever being exercised. The same end result will occur if your option finishes its contract just barely out of the money. Therefore, according to this logic, the ability of volatility to hurt you is limited, whereas its ability to help you is unlimited.

While it's good to understand the nature of the playing field you're dealing with when trading options, it does get a little more complicated when you consider the fact that your options can be sold before the expiration date to help you turn a profit or limit a loss. If the option dramatically plummets in price, and you sell it off for much less than what you paid for it, then you may find yourself wishing you'd bought a less volatile option. Generally, though, volatility is going to increase the premium of an option, because there is a greater chance that on any given day during the contract, the underlying asset will jump deep into the money and the option owner will have more chances to either sell off the option at a profit, or to exercise the option for a profit.

There are several ways to evaluate volatility. In options trading, historical volatility and implied volatility are commonly utilized metrics. *Historical volatility* refers to the observed behavior of a given financial instrument in terms of price fluctuation in the past. Implied volatility, often referred to as "IV", by contrast, is an assessment of the asset's potential for future volatility and considered by some to be the quintessential metric determining an options chance of becoming profitable.

Implied volatility is generally expressed in percentages. In his book, *The Options Course*, Harvard MBA graduate, George Fontanills claims that any implied volatility lower than 20 percent is considered low[15]. Let's see if we can witness the influence of implied volatility in the real marketplace.

---

[15] Fontanills, George A. The Options Course, Second Edition. High Profit and Low Stress Trading Methods. Hoboken, NJ. John Wiley & Sons Inc. 2005. Print.

In *Fg. 13*, look at the $105 call option, way at the bottom of the list. It's nearly $5 out of the money and will sell for about 24 cents per share. The implied volatility, which can be found in the column at the far right hand side, is 12.50 percent.

Fg. 13

Time Warner Inc. (TWX)
NYSE - NYSE Delayed Price. Currency in USD

98.77 0.00 (0.00%)
At close: 4:03PM EDT

Calls for July 20, 2018

Contract Name	Last Trade Date	Strike	Last Price	Bid	Ask	Change	% Change	Volume	Open Interest	Implied Volatility
TWX180720C00065000	2018-03-23 11:58PM EDT	65.00	29.40	25.20	29.70	0.00	-	80	80	0.00%
TWX180720C00070000	2018-01-30 4:33PM EDT	70.00	24.58	24.90	29.40	0.00	-	5	5	260.55%
TWX180720C00075000	2018-01-02 1:17PM EDT	75.00	17.50	16.70	21.20	0.00	-	5	5	0.00%
TWX180720C00080000	2018-06-14 9:30AM EDT	80.00	18.30	0.00	0.00	0.00	-	1	131	0.00%
TWX180720C00085000	2018-06-14 1:31PM EDT	85.00	14.20	0.00	0.00	0.00	-	1	288	0.00%
TWX180720C00087500	2018-06-12 10:16AM EDT	87.50	9.58	9.90	12.10	0.00	-	10	185	128.22%
TWX180720C00090000	2018-06-14 3:27PM EDT	90.00	9.10	0.00	0.00	0.00	-	136	3,848	0.00%
TWX180720C00092500	2018-06-14 3:53PM EDT	92.50	6.75	0.00	0.00	0.00	-	114	34,724	0.00%
TWX180720C00095000	2018-06-14 3:59PM EDT	95.00	4.59	0.00	0.00	0.00	-	1,285	171,957	0.00%
TWX180720C00097500	2018-06-14 3:53PM EDT	97.50	2.57	0.00	0.00	0.00	-	928	45,304	0.00%
TWX180720C00100000	2018-06-14 3:57PM EDT	100.00	1.21	0.00	0.00	0.00	-	1,003	37,335	3.13%
TWX180720C00105000	2018-06-14 3:57PM EDT	105.00	0.24	0.00	0.00	0.00	-	818	153,903	12.50%

Now, let's take a look at the more volatile HPQ call options with the same expiration date:

Fg. 14

HP Inc. (HPQ)
NYSE - NYSE Delayed Price. Currency in USD

23.53 -0.06 (-0.25%)
At close: 4:02PM EDT

Calls for July 20, 2018

Contract Name	Last Trade Date	Strike	Last Price	Bid	Ask	Change	% Change	Volume	Open Interest	Implied Volatility
HPQ180720C00017000	1969-12-31 8:00PM EDT	17.00	7.05	6.50	6.65	+7.05	+100.00%	0	0	194.53%
HPQ180720C00018000	2018-06-25 11:49AM EDT	18.00	5.30	5.50	5.60	+5.30	+100.00%	0	10	143.75%
HPQ180720C00019000	1969-12-31 8:00PM EDT	19.00	4.72	4.50	4.60	+4.72	+100.00%	0	0	118.75%
HPQ180720C00020000	2018-07-16 3:29PM EDT	20.00	3.55	3.50	3.65	+3.55	+132.96%	1	17	109.38%
HPQ180720C00021000	2018-07-17 9:32AM EDT	21.00	2.49	2.42	2.60	0.00	-	6	1,064	90.63%
HPQ180720C00022000	2018-07-12 2:23PM EDT	22.00	1.59	1.55	1.62	+1.59	+100.00%	15	1,627	57.42%
HPQ180720C00022500	2018-07-10 9:41AM EDT	22.50	1.23	1.03	1.14	+1.23	+100.00%	2	1,407	53.91%
HPQ180720C00023000	2018-07-18 3:52PM EDT	23.00	0.55	0.53	0.58	-0.16	-22.54%	186	3,428	26.17%
HPQ180720C00023500	2018-07-18 3:19PM EDT	23.50	0.14	0.15	0.17	-0.13	-48.15%	112	3,885	18.16%
HPQ180720C00024000	2018-07-18 3:53PM EDT	24.00	0.02	0.02	0.04	-0.02	-50.00%	540	5,285	21.88%
HPQ180720C00024500	2018-07-17 9:30AM EDT	24.50	0.01	0.00	0.02	0.00	-	2	215	30.08%
HPQ180720C00025000	2018-07-13 12:21PM EDT	25.00	0.01	0.00	0.01	+0.01	+100.00%	1	2,604	35.94%
HPQ180720C00026000	2018-07-16 3:30PM EDT	26.00	0.01	0.00	0.02	+0.01	+100.00%	3	114	54.69%
HPQ180720C00027000	1969-12-31 8:00PM EDT	27.00	0.01	0.00	0.02	+0.01	+100.00%	0	50	71.88%
HPQ180720C00028000	2018-07-13 11:44AM EDT	28.00	0.01	0.00	0.02	0.00	-	1	0	87.50%

If you look at the very bottom of your option chain you'll find a call option with a $28 strike price that can be had for about .02 cents per share if not cheaper. Like the TWX option, this HPQ option is about $5 out of the money. Its IV value (87.50%) is seven times that of the TWX option (12.5%). So, with such a high volatility rate, why is the HPQ option $5 out of the money but a fraction of the price of the TWX option, also $5 out of the money? The answer: scaling.

HPQ stock is worth $23.53 per share, whereas TWX is worth $65 per share. For the cheaper HPQ stock, $5 OTM is a much more significant hurdle to overcome for the option to ever be profitable, even with a higher implied volatility. The lesson here is that the volatility is scalable to the price of a stock, hence it's expressed as a percentage value.

If you look at HPQ's performance over the last year (*Fg. 15*), you'll notice that the stock did not even approach the $28 benchmark. Therefore, in order for that $28 call option to become profitable, you'd need the stock to suddenly attain that level of value by July 20th, or at least get close enough to it before July 20th that the option can be sold to another willing buyer (if you can find one). The odds of big success don't appear likely— hence, buying the call would only cost $1.00 (100 x $.01).

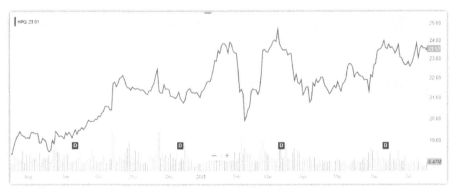

Fg. 15

Let's look at the same 1-year graph for TWX:

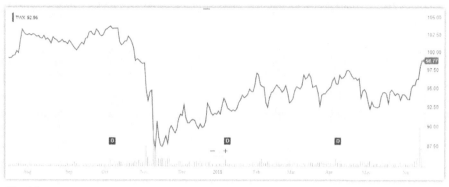

Fg. 16

Unlike HPQ, TWX spent several months over the last year within arm's length of the $5 OTM strike price ($105). Looks like things were a bit dicey back in November, but lately the stock's perked up. This option looks more attractive than the HPQ option, hence, it's more expensive. Before you pay the $24 to buy the option, you should find out why TWX plummeted in late fall 2017, and whether or not there's a decent chance for a continued short-term surge.

Thor Industries, Inc. (THO)
NYSE - NYSE Delayed Price. Currency in USD

100.98 -0.39 (-0.38%)
At close: 4:02PM EDT

Calls for July 20, 2018

Contract Name	Last Trade Date	Strike	Last Price	Bid	Ask	Change	% Change	Volume	Open Interest	Implied Volatility
THO180720C00070000	2018-06-11 1:38PM EDT	70.00	31.82	30.20	31.40	0.00	-	1	1	249.61%
THO180720C00085000	2018-07-17 10:24AM EDT	85.00	15.00	15.30	16.50	0.00	-	1	2	143.46%
THO180720C00090000	2018-07-17 10:24AM EDT	90.00	10.00	10.80	11.30	0.00	-	1	143	67.97%
THO180720C00095000	2018-07-16 12:27PM EDT	95.00	4.10	5.80	6.30	0.00	-	12	194	58.40%
THO180720C00100000	2018-07-18 2:18PM EDT	100.00	1.28	1.65	1.85	-1.24	-49.21%	14	1,525	35.84%
THO180720C00105000	2018-07-18 2:34PM EDT	105.00	0.09	0.05	0.15	-0.25	-74.29%	38	973	33.69%

Fg. 17

Let's take a look at a stock that trades at a similar price point as TWX. The Thor Industries Inc. stock (THO) is currently trading near

$100. When you locate the $105 call option for THO—(see the bottom most call option listing in *Fg. 17*.)—you'll notice that the implied volatility percentage is greater than it was with the TWX stock, 33.69% compared to 12.5%. The price of the THO option is significantly less expensive, around $.09 per share, compared to TWX's $.24 per share, all this despite THO's higher implied volatility. There must be other forces at work driving up the price of the TWX Jul 105 call. Let's take a look at THO's performance over the last year.

Fg. 18

There are a few things that stand out when looking over THO's performance over the last twelve months (within the context of the potential purchase of the Jul 105 call option). The stock traded well over $105 for much of the previous year, yet it's declined a great deal and it's not clear whether it will fall further or rebound.

It is the opinion of this author that comparatively higher price for the TWX $5 OTM call option is the due to that stock's recent surge (see *Fg. 16*). TWX looks to be on the way up, whereas few people are inclined to believe that THO is going to rebound any time soon. This perception appears to have overridden THO's more advantageous IV value.

Certain factors (such as IV) have similar impact on put options and call options. Other factors, such as recent movement of the stock price, may affect put option prices in an inverse manner relative to their effect on call options. Let's compare the call option for TWX that's ≈ $5 OTM vs. a similarly situated put option:

Time Warner Inc. (TWX)
NYSE - NYSE Delayed Price. Currency in USD

98.77 0.00 (0.00%)
At close: 4:03PM EDT

Calls for July 20, 2018

Contract Name	Last Trade Date	Strike	Last Price	Bid	Ask	Change	% Change	Volume	Open Interest	Implied Volatility
TWX180720C00105000	2018-06-14 3:57PM EDT	105.00	0.24	0.00	0.00	0.00		-	818	153,903	12.50%

Puts for July 20, 2018

Contract Name	Last Trade Date	Strike	Last Price	Bid	Ask	Change	% Change	Volume	Open Interest	Implied Volatility
TWX180720P00095000	2018-06-14 3:11PM EDT	95.00	0.70	0.00	0.00	0.00		-	317	36,350	12.50%

Fg. 19

In the image above you can see that though implied volatility is identical, the most recent put option sold for more than the most recent call option. There is no obvious explanation here that is consistent with our previous analysis. Given that we noted a price surge in *Fg. 16*, a put option should be worth less than the call option of similar *moneyness*. Maybe we're missing something. Or maybe we're zeroing in on a great buying opportunity!

Options traders largely rely on the strategy of searching for discrepancies. One discrepancy that's rather easy to screen for is the difference between a stock's historical volatility and its implied volatility. If an options trader can spot an option with an implied volatility that's too low given its historical volatility, then that option is said to be cheap and may prove to be a good deal. If the historical volatility indicates that an option's implied volatility is too high, then the option is thought to be expensive and should be sold if possible. Traders are also looking for mismatches between the implied volatility of an option and the volatility of its underlying asset. If the asset is more volatile than the options with which IV credits it, then you've got an option worth buying. If the asset is more stable than is reflected by the IV, sell it away[16].

---

[16] Fontanills, George A. The Options Course, Second Edition. High Profit and Low Stress Trading Methods. Hoboken, NJ. John Wiley & Sons Inc. 2005. Print.

Implied volatility is a concept that you understand more the more often you use it. As Michael Sincere says, "To demonstrate how difficult it is to define, I'd like you to answer a question. Can you define gravity?" Sincere goes on to offer a very psychologically-focused explanation of implied volatility: "It's the urgency, or expectation, that the stock price might undergo a big change that drives traders to bid-up the options (forcing both the premium and implied volatility higher).[17]"

Fg. 20

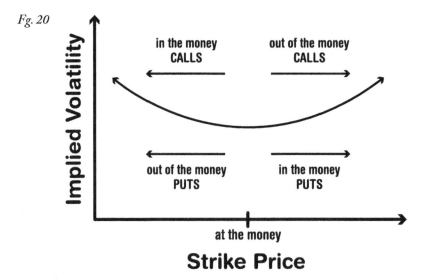

Fg. 20 : Another macro-trend in option volatility is the tendency of options to become more volatile as they become moreso in or out of the money-- this is known as the volatility smile or grin.

Interest Rates & Dividends

Though interest rates and dividends aren't as important as the other factors influencing options pricing, they still must be acknowledged. When interest rates (the cost of borrowing money) go up, the price of calls generally increase and puts decrease. The opposite is true when interest rates go down.

---

[17] Sincere, Michael. *Understanding Options*. New York: McGraw Hill, 2014. Electronic book.

When dividends of the underlying asset increase, the price of calls decrease and the price of puts increase. When dividends decrease, the opposite occurs[18]. We won't get into the specific mechanisms of these rather negligible factors in this text.

The next chapter drills down even further on option evaluation metrics by offering information about the "Greeks."

---

[18] http://www.investopedia.com/university/options-pricing/option-price-influence.asp

| 5 |

Win at Options By Speaking Greek

It wouldn't be a book on options trading without the inevitable foray into the world of the Greeks. The **Greeks** refer to several key metrics denoted by a Greek letter, only a small handful—delta, gamma, theta, vega, and rho—are in the vocabulary of the typical options trader, with delta being the most useful.

Fg. 21

Delta

Part of what makes delta useful is that it's quite easy to understand. As we explained in Chapter 2, if you buy an option and suddenly the underlying stock spikes in the right direction, it's more advantageous (and usually more profitable) to resell the option than execute the option. What the delta metric does is tell you how much the price of your option is expected to move when the underlying stock moves by a single point. Though the data provided from delta isn't iron clad, it can prove to be an extremely useful reference point when trying to gauge the potential profitability of an option.

Deltas are always going to have an absolute value between 0 and 1, though traders often drop the decimal place—saying the option has a 50 delta, as opposed to a .5 delta. Calls always have a positive delta and puts, a negative delta.

Usually the delta is given, especially on brokerage sites or exchange websites that specialize in options trading, but it's also easy to calculate the delta for an option. All you need is snapshots of the both the stock's value and the option's value. Take a call option, for instance. Let's say the stock is on the market for $30, and there's a call option with two months to go before expiration that's currently ATM (at the money) and a $30 call contract that may currently be purchased for $1 per share. When the stock goes up in value, let's say to $32, the call option is also going to become more valuable. (In this case the call option is suddenly $2 in the money.) Let's say that the call option goes from $1 per share to $2 per share. <u>The delta of the option is calculated by dividing the change in the option price by the change in the stock price.</u> In this example you get 1 divided by 2, or .5. This is commonly referred to as a "50 delta."

Fg. 22

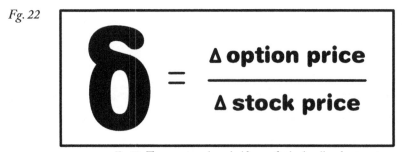

Fg. 22 : The equation above holds true for both call and put options.

Using this formula, you can see why calculating the delta value of a put option always results in a negative number. As the price of the stock goes up, the value of the put option always goes down, so you always end up dividing a negative number by a positive number, or vice versa, resulting in a negative delta value.

> *Note : Another common principle of delta that's illustrated in the example above is that once the option is ITM, it's usually going to have a delta value between .5 and 1.0. The opposite is also true. If the call option is out of the money, then it's probably going to have a delta value between 0 and .5. Furthermore, the value of delta changes dramatically as the end of the option contract nears. For in the money options near the end of their contracts, delta values are very close to 1. For out of the money options near the end of the contract, delta values are very close to zero.*

Fg. 23

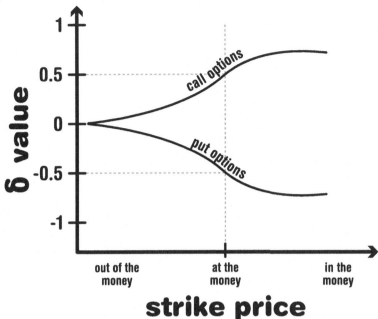

Using Delta to Prevent Common Frustrations

One of the things that frustrates beginner-level options traders, and may turn them off to options entirely, is purchasing an option and watching the stock value move $2 or even $3 in the "right" direction only to find that the value of the option has barely changed. Many beginners first approaching the options market may be drawn to the very inexpensive, out of the money option contracts with very little time left on the contracts. Sure you can get one of these contracts for $20, but it's not likely to make you any money. The reason for this is that the delta value of out of the money option contracts near the point of expiration is close to zero. Even if the stock moves significantly toward the money, the option may not gain any significant value. A lot of these extremely cheap, nearly expired OTM options are the equivalents of a Hail Mary pass. Learning how to read an option's delta value can spare you from this frustration.

Fg. 24

Gamma

Gamma measures the expected change of the delta value in relation to a $1 change in the price of a stock. Remember, the delta value is anything but constant throughout the life of an option, but the extent to which it fluctuates may hinge on a few different factors, such as the proximity to the option's expiration date.

> *Note : When the expiration date approaches, the gamma value is high, because small changes in the price of the stock can dramatically change the delta value. In "Options for the Beginner and Beyond," Edward Olmstead uses the example of a call option that's slightly OTM and very close to expiration. The delta value for the option may be close to zero, but a small change bringing the stock slightly into the money may result in a delta value close to one. Thus, the stock, at this point has a higher gamma value[19].*

For the beginner-level options trader, the most important thing to understand about the gamma metric is the concept of ***gamma risk***. If your gamma level is high and you're in a position to make a profit or minimize loss by selling or exercising your option, then you may be wise to do so since the option could quickly deteriorate.

Though gamma analysis is used by the pros, especially in risk assessments, it's not essential that you have a thorough understanding of how to leverage this metric when you're just starting out. The bottom line of the gamma metric is that when gamma increases, the prices of your options are more sensitive to changes in the price of the stock.

---

[19] Olmstead, Edward. Options for the Beginner and Beyond. Upper Saddle River, NJ: FT Prentice Hall. 2006. Print.

Fg. 25

Theta

Theta measures the price change of an option in relation to a unit of time (usually a day). As you know by now, the closer an option gets to its expiration date, the less value it tends to have—all other factors being equal. What the theta metric does is quantify the extent to which this value is changing on a day-by-day basis. Theta, therefore, is a negative value. This lost value, in options jargon, is often referred to as "theta decay."

For a beginner, you should understand that theta decay detracts from the value of an option at an ever increasing rate. If you've got an option you're thinking about selling, and there are three weeks or so left in the contract, be prepared for the theta decay to make a serious dent in the value of your option. The closer you get to your expiration date, the more severe the theta decay.

In Options for Beginners, Edward Olmstead offers an illustration on theta decay using simple square roots. He says, "The magnitude of theta for an at-the-money option varies inversely as the square root of the time remaining until expiration[20]." That may seem like a bit of a mouth full, but when you consider it within the context of a real scenario it's a bit clearer.

> *Note (advanced) : For example—if I have an ATM option that's going to expire in 45 days, its theta decay will proceed at 1/3 the speed relative to the same option at the money, with only 5 days remaining on the contract. This can be calculated by dividing 45 by 5 (= 9) then taking the inverse of the square root (3) to get 1/3.*

---

[20] Olmstead, Edward. Options for the Beginner and Beyond. Upper Saddle River, NJ: FT Prentice Hall. 2006. Print.

Again, if you can't get your head fully around theta yet, just know that the time decay becomes more impactful the closer the option comes to expiring. Also understand, however, that theta is never the end all/be all that determines the value of your options. Any investor should realize from the moment she purchases an option that it's going to start going down in value and that, in order for the option to prove profitable, the underlying asset must move in the right direction with a decent magnitude of delta force behind it (assuring that the option price will move in the right direction as well).

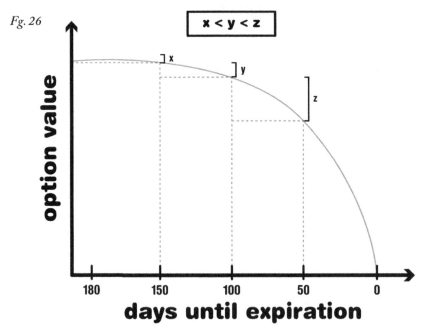

Fg. 26

Fg. 26 : The pace at which an option's value deteriorates becomes quicker and quicker as the option's expiration date approaches.

Vega

We don't have an image of the Greek letter vega, because vega is not a real Greek letter. Vega indicates the amount of change expected in an option price for every percent change in implied volatility. Remember, options with underlying assets perceived to be highly volatile tend to be more expensive than options with more stable underlying assets. Vega is meant to show the specific degree to which changes in implied volatility may affect the price of an option.

Fg. 27

Rho

The final Greek we will discuss is Rho, which is considered by the experts to be the least important of all the Greeks[21]. Rho measures the effect of interest rates (on US treasury bills) on the pricing of options. The Rho metric can be either negative (for puts) or positive (calls). As of the writing of this book (2015), interest rates are so low that the Rho metric is negligible.

[21] Sincere, Michael. *Understanding Options*. New York: McGraw Hill, 2014. Electronic book.

| 6 |
Popular Options Strategies

As stated previously, you're not going to automatically profit on an option just because your option is ITM. You also have to account for the amount you paid to own the option. Traders use a concept called a "breakeven point" to help them clarify when they're actually holding a profitable option.

For calls, your breakeven point can be calculated simply by adding your strike price to the premium you paid to own the option. If I own a $49 call option on a stock worth $50 (already ITM), and I paid $2 a share to own this option, then my breakeven point is equal to $49+$2 or $51. Once the stock rises above $51, then and only then is my option truly profitable.

> *Note : For the purpose of this discussion, assume that the options are being held to the point of expiration. In the scenario above, there is, of course, a way to turn a profit, even without the stock reaching its breakeven point. For instance, if the stock rises to $51, then the price of the option will probably spike up higher than the $2 you paid for it, and you can then sell the option to another party at a profit before the stock even reaches the breakeven point.*

Here's an example of how utilizing the breakeven point is helpful when assessing and monitoring options strategy:

Chapter 3 discussed selling the covered call option, whereby an option is sold on a stock you own, one that you're comfortable selling at a certain price. You used DuPont, which was trading at $32.18, and you sold a covered call option with a strike price of $35. You sold the option for about $.50 per share. Using this strategy, in order for the party who bought your option to reach his breakeven point, the price of DuPont would have to climb to at least $35.50 before the expiration period. Now, from the perspective of your position, and, assuming that you're truly committed to unloading all of your DuPont stock, there is another breakeven point that you need to keep in mind. You collected $50 (.50 x 100) from the sale of the $35 call option, and, as the owner of 100 shares of DuPont, you're losing $50 every time the stock declines by $.50. Therefore, as the writer/seller of the covered call, your breakeven point is the price you paid for the stock, $32.18, minus the per-share price of the call option ($.50)—$31.68. In other words, even if you pad your coffers by selling the call option, your DuPont play is still going to lose money if you end up getting out at $31.68 or lower.

Straddling a Stock Using Options

The *straddle* tactic is both easy to understand and potentially useful for investors who believe that they can spot interesting trends in the market. In Chapter 4, we took a look at the WWE stock when trying

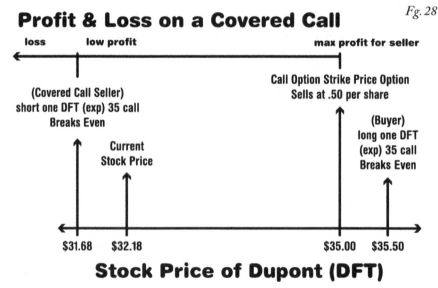

Fg. 28

Profit & Loss on a Covered Call

loss   low profit   max profit for seller

(Covered Call Seller) short one DFT (exp) 35 call **Breaks Even**

Call Option Strike Price Option Sells at .50 per share

Current Stock Price

(Buyer) long one DFT (exp) 35 call **Breaks Even**

$31.68 $32.18 $35.00 $35.50

Stock Price of Dupont (DFT)

Fg. 28: In the example above, "(exp)" is used as a stand-in for any given expiration month.

to assess implied volatility and its effect on the pricing of options. Every late March or early April, the WWE brings its signature product, "Wrestlemania", to the market. There's always a whole lot of talk about whether the current year's Wrestlemania is going to be a successful event, and in the aftermath of the spectacle major changes are revealed that affect the direction of the company, most notably, who is going to be the WWE's new champion, as well as who's going to be retiring or who's going to be coming back or stepping up to a bigger role. If you look at the WWE's stock performance chart over the last five years (*Fg. 29*), you'll notice that there are some significant fluctuations in the stock's price occurring between the months of March and May. For the sake of argument, let's say that you can't pinpoint whether or not Wrestlemania leads to the plummeting of the stock's value or raises it, but you're quite certain that it changes it in some particular way, and dramatically.

In this event, you might consider using a straddle strategy. In a straddle, a put and a call option are purchased for the same stock at the same strike price. Let's say that next February the WWE stock is trading at around $90 per share. You decide to straddle the stock by purchasing an ATM call and an ATM put option. Each option costs you

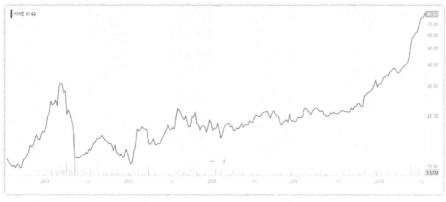

Fg. 29

two dollars per share to purchase, so you've technically invested $400 if you're buying, so you've technically invested $200 if you're buying standard 100 share put and call contracts. You know that Wrestlemania is on April third this year, so you select the third Friday in April for your expiration date. Now, in order for you to make money on your straddle, the WWE stock needs to be either above $94 ($4 above $90) or below $86 ($4 below $90) by the end of the contract. Hence, breakeven points on the straddle strategy are expressed as two limits: above x or below y or beyond the range of x to y. In straddle plays, you need higher implied volatility to have a good chance to pass the breakeven point, but, unfortunately, as always, options with higher implied volatility are likely to prove to be expensive. Furthermore, whenever a company is about to release big news or put a significant product on the market for the first time, the price of all options associated with that stock are inclined to spike somewhat in anticipation of some major movement.

Fg. 30

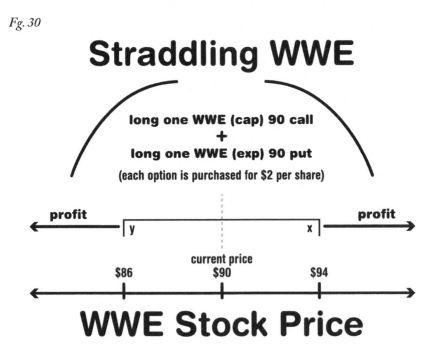

Straddling WWE

long one WWE (cap) 90 call
+
long one WWE (exp) 90 put
(each option is purchased for $2 per share)

profit   profit

y   x

current price
$86 $90 $94

WWE Stock Price

The Strangle

The *strangle* strategy is like the straddle except the call and the put are set to different prices, usually with the put strike price being lower. Investors generally turn to the strangle when they'd rather pay a little bit less in premiums while betting that the stock will move well past the breakeven point for either option. For example, General Motors is trading at $33. You decide to pursue a strangle strategy by purchasing a cheap OTM call option with a strike price of $36. The call costs you 50 cents per share in premiums. You concurrently purchase a cheap put option with a strike price of $31, and you pay $1 per share. Your total (combined) premium payment is $1.50. Therefore, in order to break even on the strangle, you need General Motors to rise above $37.50 ($36 + $1.50) or drop below $29.50 ($31-$1.50). Just as with your straddle strategy, the strangle strategy should be driven on the assumption that a stock is going to change in price, either up or down (you're not sure which). A strangle will give you more options than a straddle and will also give the investor a chance to enter into a market position for potentially less money.

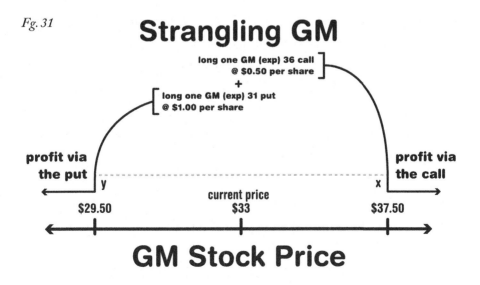

Fg. 31

Strangling GM

long one GM (exp) 36 call
@ $0.50 per share
+
long one GM (exp) 31 put
@ $1.00 per share

profit via the put

profit via the call

y
current price
$33
x

$29.50

$37.50

GM Stock Price

A Bull (or Bear) Spread

The vertical spread refers to the simultaneous purchase and sale of calls or puts on the same stock at different strike prices. As with the previous two strategies, the purpose of the *spread* is to provide the investor with flexibility of positioning. Let's reuse the General Motors example, assuming the stock is still trading at about $33. If you decide to buy a call on GM with a strike price of $35 and sell a call with a strike price of $37, you're still going to end up paying an overall net premium, as the $35 call option that you bought is more expensive than the $37 option that you sold. For the purpose of this illustration, let's assume that you paid $.50 to buy your $35 call and that you sold your $37 call for $.20. Therefore, your total premium payment to establish your current position is $.30.

Note : For call spreads such as this one, it's not necessary to own the stock. In the event that the $37 call gets exercised, you will have presumably already exercised your $35 call.

In order for your spread to pass the breakeven point, the stock must rise higher than $35.30 ($35 + .30). If the stock ends up at any point between $35.30 and $37 (within the spread), then the $37 call will not be exercised and you'll take a profit. Should the stock soar above $37 and you're forced to oblige the call you sold, then your profit will cap out at $1.70 ($37-$35.30) regardless of how much higher the stock surges above $37. In other words, even if the stock soars to $40 or higher, for all intents and purposes, in your universe, the stock ended up at $37, as you are pre-obliged to sell the stock at this price.

The moral of the story on spreads is that they allow you to cut down on the expense of your premiums, but they limit, to an extent, your capacity for profit. Spreads are very popular among professional investors who would gladly trade away a shot-in-the-dark chance at seeing an enormous profit if it means cutting down on their risk.

Fg. 32

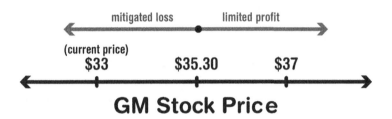

The Bull Spread

**long one GM (exp) 35 call @ $.50 per share
+ short one GM (exp) 37 call @ $.20 per share**

Total Position = $.30 per share

mitigated loss limited profit

(current price)
$33 **$35.30** **$37**

GM Stock Price

The trade illustrated in *Fg. 32* in which two calls are concurrently bought and sold at different strike prices is known as a bull spread, as the investor needs the stock to behave bullishly (go up) in order to see a profit.

A bear spread can be executed by simultaneously purchasing and selling put options on the same stock at different strike prices. Just like in the bull spread, you're trading limited profitability for a less expensive premium.

Here's a list of several other strategies for your consideration. Your broker can enlighten you as to whether or not they'd work for you and, of course, you can virtually practice them until you're comfortable with attempting them for real.

The Cash-Secured Put

The cash-secured put is used by investors who are looking to acquire ownership of a stock, but want to get in with minimal expenditure. To accomplish this, the investor writes a put option that's slightly

OTM. If the stock doesn't go down in price and the put option is not assigned, then the investor pockets the premium and may write/sell another put option. When the stock waxes bearish, the investor purchases the underlying stock near the strike price and hopes that the stock turns quickly bullish before his new acquisition is assigned via the put option. The main idea of the cash-secured put is to use premium revenues from the sale of the put option to mitigate the cost of acquiring the sought-after stock.

The Married Put

A married put weds long stock with a long put to provide protection for the investor. For this strategy, you purchase the stock and the put at the same time. This strategy functions like an insurance policy and provides a "floor" should the asset's price plunge suddenly and drastically. Experts say the married put provides the investor with limited risk and unlimited reward. As with many strategies, timing is key, but with the married put you can protect yourself against potential short-term losses.

Fg. 33

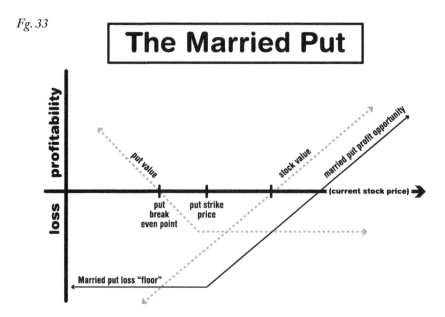

The Protective Collar

The protective collar strategy occurs when an investor purchases an out-of-the-money (OTM) put option and writes an OTM call option at the same time for the same underlying asset (i.e. shares of stock). This strategy works best after a long position in a stock has produced significant gains and is the perfect way to lock in profit without selling your shares. Try to purchase the stock and the put during low-volatility conditions for the best outcome. This allows you to buy longer-term protection.

Fg. 34

The Protective Collar

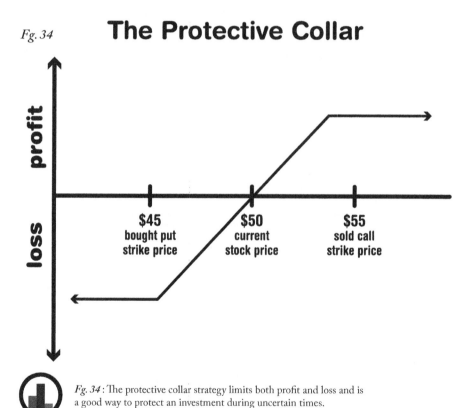

Fg. 34 : The protective collar strategy limits both profit and loss and is a good way to protect an investment during uncertain times.

The Butterfly Spread

According to Dr. Joe Duarte,cite the Butterfly Spread combines the aforementioned bull put spread and bear put spread expiring the same month for a debit. The image of the butterfly is used because the two short puts possess the same strike price and are said to make up the body of the butterfly. Conversely, the two long puts include different strike prices (above and below the proverbial "body") and they are said to be the wings. This strategy provides limited risk with limited reward and can get expensive due to the trading costs associated with the three positions involved. However, it's an interesting strategy and one that's good to try on paper as you practice your options trading.

Fg. 35

The Long Put Butterfly Spread

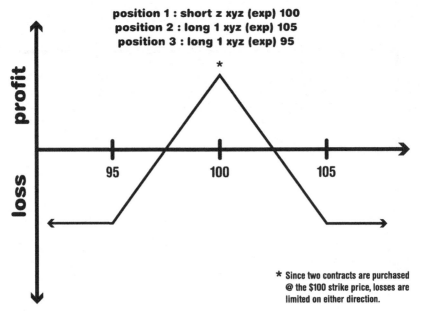

position 1 : short z xyz (exp) 100
position 2 : long 1 xyz (exp) 105
position 3 : long 1 xyz (exp) 95

* Since two contracts are purchased @ the $100 strike price, losses are limited on either direction.

Fg. 35 : The butterfly spread strategy is useful when a stock appears to be stable within a certain price range

The Iron Condor

While we're discussing winged creatures…the Iron Condor involves an investor holding both a long and a short position in two different strangle scenarios. This is a fairly complex strategy that is not meant for the beginner as it takes time to master. However, once you're ready to exceed the safe havens of covered calls and other beginner strategies, and if you're someone who really enjoys "having some skin in the game", you'll love the excitement of the Iron Condor. When you're ready, ask your broker about it and, again, practice it on paper until you feel confident about the particulars.

Fg. 36

Iron Condor

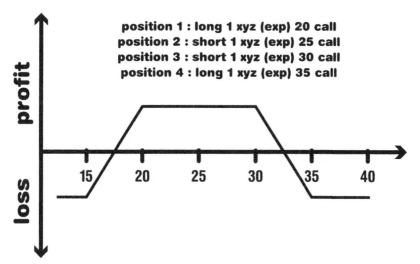

position 1 : long 1 xyz (exp) 20 call
position 2 : short 1 xyz (exp) 25 call
position 3 : short 1 xyz (exp) 30 call
position 4 : long 1 xyz (exp) 35 call

Fg. 36 : The iron condor combines multiple strategies into one giving the investor a wide but limited range in which to profit

Remember, NO strategy is risk free. All carry different degrees of reward and risk, and you need to decide – as you progress – whether you wish to continue to play it safe or if you're willing (and can afford) to be a little more aggressive in your investments. A broker who has your best interests in mind should be able to lead you in the right direction in regards to testing different strategies. If you trust him – and you should only maintain a broker you trust – go with his advice.

Rolling Positions

The term "rolling" refers to one of the most common ways to adjust an option's position. You can roll either a long or a short option position, but in order to stay in tune with the beginner-level knowledge in this book, we'll focus on rolling the *short position*.

Understand, first of all, that with rolling, there are no guarantees. As with everything you do in the options market, you are "speculating" and hoping that the moves you make result in a profit rather than a loss. Whenever you roll a short position, you're buying back an option you initially sold--thereby closing that position--and writing/selling a new option on the same stock but with a different strike price, thereby opening a new position.

Let's take a look at three of the more basic types of rolling positions:

Rolling the Covered Call

When you choose to roll a covered call, you go in the "up and out" direction. You're looking to go "up" in strike price and to go "out" in time. This way you balance the decrease in premium you'd encounter for selling a higher OTM strike price in contrast to the greater premium you'd receive for selling an option that is further from its expiration date. Here's an example:

Suppose you select a buy-to-close order for the front-month 80-strike call. At the exact same time, you sell to open an out-of-the-money 85-strike call (this is "rolling up") that expires in 60 days (this is referred to as "rolling out"). Due to higher time value, the back-month 85-strike call is trading for $2.50. So, you pay $2.30 to buy back the front-month call and receive $2.50 for the back-month call. Hence, you do this trade for a net credit of $0.20 ($2.50 sale price - $2.30 purchase price) or a total of $20.

There are positives and negatives here and maybe some things that make you a bit nervous. On one hand, since you raised the strike price of the option to $85, you can potentially make more profit on the stock since the obligation was originally at $80. You had to buy back the first-month call for more money than you received when selling it, BUT you covered that cost by selling the back-month strike call for more premium.

The risk is present because there are two months left before the expiration date of the new options, and you have no idea what might happen with the price of the stock during that period of time. It may proceed in your favor…but you might see a loss as well. Remember, there's time for the market to move in a direction that won't be to your advantage. You have to decide whether or not it's worth taking that chance.

Rolling a Cash-Secured Put

In this scenario, you want to roll "down and out" in order to avoid assignment. This is converse to the "up and out" direction you want to go when rolling the covered call. Here's an example:

You're going to sell a 30-day cash-secured put on your favorite stock, Melody Musical Instruments. It has a strike price of $50. When the stock was trading at $52, you received a premium of $.80 per share for selling the put option. However, the stock is now trading at only $49.50, and it's getting close to the expiration date. You're worried. So, you need to be sure to avoid assignment by buying back that front-month 50-strike put and, therefore, cancel your obligation. However, that front-month put you sold way back when for $.80 is now selling for $1.45.

So, what can you do to accomplish the roll? You need to enter a buy-to-close order for the front-month 50-strike put. In the same trade, you need to sell to open a back-month 48.50-strike put (this is the rolling down part), 90 days from expiration (rolling out) which is trading for $1.70. By doing this, you receive a net credit of $0.25 ($1.70-$1.45) or a total of $25.

The increase in time value of the 90-day option therefore allows you to roll for a net credit of $25 even though the back-month put is further out-of-the-money. The caveat? Whenever you do a down and out roll, you might take a loss on the front-month put. In addition, you're not sure in what direction the market will move in the months before the expiration, so you really haven't secured any gains on the back-month put, which exposes you to further risk. Hence, you should always do a down and out roll for the shortest possible time period.

Rolling a Short Call Spread

Similar to rolling individual options, you can roll a spread by moving strike prices up or down and moving out in time. However, with a spread, there are generally four options to be traded during the process (closing two and opening two) instead of just two. This, in itself, makes it a little more complicated right off the bat.

Remember that favorite stock... Melody Musical Instruments? Well, now it's trading at $53 and you're in a bearish position. Your broker advises you to sell a 55/60 short call spread 30 days from expiration time. As such, let's say you're going to receive a net credit of $1.00. But now the stock is heading upwards and is selling at $55.50. There are only 15 days left until the expiration date and, sadly, the cost to buy back the spread has risen to $1.70.

You think that this is just a fluke, and your research shows that this stock is going to go back down. So, you decide to roll up and out. That means you're rolling up in strike price and out in expiration time.

So, you buy back the 55/60 short call spread for $1.70 and, at the same exact time, sell another short call spread that has a short strike of 60, a long strike of 65, and is 45 days from expiration. As a result, you receive a credit of $1.10. You wind up with a net debit of -$.60. However, if the stock is below $60 by the time you reach the new expiration date, you'll be back in the money to the tune of $.40. (That's the $1.00 net credit to open the 55/60 spread minus the $1.70 net credit to close it, plus the $1.10 net credit to open the new 60/65 spread.)

Sound complicated? It is! And, remember, your forecasts about the direction of the stock prices need to be on-the-mark if you're going to navigate this roll successfully. You should definitely ditch instead of roll if you're not confident in your predictions.

Note : These are all advanced techniques that you needn't try if they make you uncomfortable. There are plenty of other ways to make money in options – ways that are fraught with a whole lot less risk. Again, if you wish to try these, do them on paper first so you can truly understand the pitfalls.

conclusion

As was stated in the introduction of this book, options trading has been in use in some form for thousands of years. All of the principles that you've learned here (and will learn elsewhere) about successful options trading aren't limited to stocks. The CBOE and other exchanges offer opportunities to buy and sell options for a myriad of other securities such as currencies, exchange traded funds, mutual funds, futures, commodities, and more. If you already hold a fair degree of market expertise in any of these areas, then you'll be able to apply your knowledge in the options trade.

In his *Trading Options for Dummies*, Dr. Joe Duarte offers these tips for staying on the right course as you continue to navigate an investment world that can be both risky and confusing. He suggests you remember these four things:

- **Get Approval** : Remember, you must always get approval from your broker to begin trading options. This is an SEC rule! If you are granted approval, it means that your financial situation matches the requirements for options trading. New traders will most likely get approved for basic option strategies only.

- **Practice** : As with trading stocks, you can "paper trade" options as well. This will provide you with knowledge without risk and prepare you to enter the "real world" of options trading. Practice until you're comfortable with the basic strategies.

- **Be Disciplined** : Keep abreast of the items in your portfolio and follow YOUR rules for each trade you've made. For example, if you enter a trade with an intention of not holding it for longer than a month, stick it your guns and proceed in that direction.

- **Keep Track of the expiration dates** : Essential to managing the position of an option is knowing the expiration date. At first, when you're only dealing with a trade or two, this might not be too difficult, but once you get in deep, you'll need to devise a system to keep track of each expiration date.

What we've hopefully accomplished through the writing of this book is a summary-level description of the essential mechanics of options trading. As you can probably infer, there are a whole lot more (and more complex) options trading strategies available beyond the world of spreads, strangles, and straddles. There are also many great resources you can access which catalog other strategies and methods for managing a successful options trade. If you're interested in some of the higher-level, applied math strategies that can help you learn how to form fine calculations on risk and earnings potential, then check out Simon Vine's book, Options Trading Strategy and Risk Management. If you're looking for a near savant or "quant" level look at options, then check out C.B. Reehl's The Mathematics of Options Trading.

Don't, however, let a distaste for complex mathematics dissuade you from exploring the options market. There are plenty of successful traders who do just fine using sound, fundamental, sensible and simple knowledge. Good luck... and have fun!

glossary

American-Style Option-
An option that may be exercised at any point prior to the expiration date.

Ask Price-
A price that a particular party is willing to take in exchange for a stock or some other security.

Bid Price-
A price that a particular party is willing to pay to obtain a stock or some other security.

Call-
An option that guarantees the "owner" the right to purchase a stock at a certain price (strike price) before a specified expiration date.

Covered Call-
When a trader selling a call option owns the requisite shares in the underlying asset and is therefore able to readily produce the shares if the option is "called in".

Cost Basis-
The cost basis for a stock is the original cost of obtaining the stock adjusted for revenue obtained through the stock, such as dividends, capital distribution, and any revenues gained from selling options on the stock.

Chicago Board Options Exchange (CBOE)-
The first trading exchange to legitimize and regulate the trading of stock options.

European-Style Option-
An option that may only be exercised on the exact date of expiration.

Gamma Risk-
A level of risk affecting the profit/loss of an option, whereby small changes in the value of the underlying asset may drastically reduce the delta value of the stock, leaving the investor in a position in which a small change can significantly eliminate or diminish profit.

Greeks-
A collection of metrics used to describe the anticipated behavior of option value in response to various factors such as changes in the underlying value (delta), changes in time (theta), changes in interest rates (rho), changes in volatility (vega) and anticipated changes in the delta value (gamma).

Historical Volatility-
The observed volatility of a particular financial instrument as observed by past performance. (Contrast with "implied volatility")

Implied Volatility-
An important measurement of an options value that predicts the volatility in price for an option. The higher the implied volatility, the more likely that the stock will dramatically change in value. Distinct from historical volatility in that implied volatility attempts to predict future behavior, whereas historical volatility is an evaluation of past behavior.

In The Money (ITM)-
When an option's strike price will yield immediate intrinsic value. A call option is ITM when the strike price is lower than the actual value of the underlying asset. A put option is ITM when the strike price is higher than the actual value of the underlying asset.

Intrinsic Value-
The amount by which a call option's strike price is lower than the underlying asset price, or the amount by which a put option's strike price is higher than the underlying asset price. An option with intrinsic value can be exercised for a profit if and only if the premium paid to obtain the option is less than the intrinsic value.

Long Position-
In stock trading, a long position refers to the holding of any stock or derivative that will increase in value when the stock goes up.

Limit order-
When a trader agrees to purchase a certain financial asset at or below a certain price. A limit order is usually set at a price somewhere in between the ask price and the bid price.

Moneyness-
The difference between an option's set strike price and the price of the underlying asset or stock, or the extent to which an option is in or out of the money. Moneyness profoundly influences the pricing of options.

Naked Call Writing-
When a trader selling a call option does not own the requisite shares in the underlying asset and is therefore not able to readily produce the shares if the option is "called in."

Naked Put-
When a trader purchases a put (the right to sell a stock at a certain price) without actually owning the underlying stock.

Options Clearing Corporation (OCC)-
A corporation formed by the Chicago Board Options Exchange responsible for ensuring that options contracts are enforced.

Options Chain-
A price listing of call and put options at various strike prices and expiration dates.

Out of the Money (OTM)-
A call option is out of the money when the value of the stock is lower than the strike price. A put option is out of the money when the value of the stock is higher than the strike price.

Owner-
The party in an options contract entitled to exercise the option. (Compare with "Writer.")

Premium-
The price paid to own a stock option.

Put-
An option that guarantees the "owner" the right to sell a stock at a certain price (strike price) before a specified expiration date.

Short Position-
In stock trading, a short position refers to the holding of any stock or derivative that will increase in value when the stock goes down.

Spread -
An option investment strategy whereby a call (or put) is simultaneously bought and sold creating a cheaper overall premium price while limiting profitability to a certain extent.

Stock Option-
A contract guaranteeing the right to purchase (call) or sell (put) a specific stock at specific price within a specific period of time.

Straddle-
An options investment strategy whereby a put and a call option are purchased for the same stock at the same strike price.

Strangle-
An option investment strategy whereby a put and call option are purchased for the same stock but at different strike prices, usually with the put strike price being lower and the call price being higher.

Strike Price-
A price that's specified in an options contract at which the buyer of the option may purchase a stock (in a call) or sell a stock (in a put) within the period specified by the contract.

Time Decay-
The phenomenon of an option losing value over time.

Time Value-
An element that contributes to the overall valuation of an option on the basis of the amount of time remaining in an option contract prior to the expiration date, the more time remaining in the contract, the more valuable the option.

Underlying Asset-
The asset from which an option is derived. With stock options, stocks are the underlying assets.

Volatility-
The propensity of a certain financial instrument to significantly fluctuate in value over time.

Wasting Asset-
An asset that declines in value over time. Because options lose value the closer they get to their expiration dates, they are considered to be wasting assets.

Writer-
The party in an options contract obliged to buy or sell a stock when the owner exercises an option. (Compare with "Owner.")

about clydebank

We are a multi-media publishing company that provides reliable, high-quality, and easily accessible information to a global customer base. Developed out of the need for beginner-friendly content that can be accessed across multiple platforms, we deliver unbiased, up-to-date, information through our multiple product offerings.

Through our strategic partnerships with some of the world's largest retailers, we are able to simplify the learning process for customers around the world, providing our readers with an authoritative source of information for the subjects that matter to them. Our end-user focused philosophy puts the satisfaction of our customers at the forefront of our mission. We are committed to creating multi-media products that allow our customers to learn what they want, when they want, and how they want.

ClydeBank Finance is a division of the multimedia-publishing firm ClydeBank Media. ClydeBank Media's goal is to provide affordable, accessible information to a global market through different forms of media such as eBooks, paperback books and audio books. Company divisions are based on subject matter, each consisting of a dedicated team of researchers, writers, editors and designers.

For more information, please visit us at :
www.clydebankmedia.com
or contact *info@clydebankmedia.com*

notes

REMEMBER TO DOWNLOAD YOUR FREE DIGITAL ASSETS!

Visit the URL below to access your free Digital Asset files that are included with the purchase of this book.

☑ Summaries   ☑ White Papers
☑ Cheat Sheets   ☑ Charts & Graphs
☑ Articles   ☑ Reference Materials

DOWNLOAD YOURS HERE:

www.clydebankmedia.com/options-assets

Explore the World of
FINANCE

AdoptAClassroom.org

ClydeBank Media is a Proud Sponsor of

AdoptAClassroom.org

AdoptAClassroom.org empowers teachers by providing the classroom supplies and materials needed to help their students learn and succeed. As an award-winning 501(c)(3), AdoptAClassroom.org makes it easy for individual donors and corporate sponsors to donate funds to K-12 classrooms in public, private and charter schools throughout the U.S.

On average, teachers spend $600 of their own money each year to equip their classrooms – 20% of teachers spend more than $1000 annually. Since 1998 AdoptAClassroom.org has raised more than $30 million and benefited more than 4.25 million students. AdoptAClassroom.org holds a 4-star rating from Charity Navigator.

TO LEARN MORE, VISIT ADOPTACLASSROOM.ORG

Made in the USA
Coppell, TX
29 January 2021